OUR AMISH NEIGHBORS

OUI

ᴀMISH NEIGHBORS

WILLIAM I. SCHREIBER

DRAWINGS BY
SYBIL GOULD

WILLIAM I. SCHREIBER
THE COLLEGE OF WOOSTER, WOOSTER, OHIO

Our Amish Neighbors

AWARDS

— Chosen by the American Library Association as one of the best books of the year (1963).

— Shared the Folklore Prize given by the University of Chicago.

— Top Honor Designation by the Fourteenth Annual Exhibit of Chicago and Midwestern Bookmaking.

First published by the University of Chicago Press, ©1962
10 printings

To My Four Sons Who Have Grown Up with
Our Amish Neighbors
William, James, Ralph, Stephen
and to Their Mother
Clare Adel Schreiber

ACKNOWLEDGMENTS

A few rare books emerge from an author's study, the products of a single creative mind and effort. *Our Amish Neighbors* is not one of these. I have had the help of many friends and colleagues. I recall with gratitude the following persons and would like here to express my appreciation for their assistance over the years:

The late Theodore Brenson, formerly of the College of Wooster and the Metropolitan Museum of New York, who first suggested the Amish as a subject.

The late Howard W. Elkinton, former editor of the *American-German Review* (Carl Schurz Foundation publication, Philadelphia), for printing my first observations on the Amish.

The late Otto H. Lehman, former Ohio legislator, who first introduced me to a Mennonite church service.

John B. Garver, for permission to browse in "The World's Largest Country Store" in Strasburg, Ohio.

Dr. Howard Foster Lowry, president of the College of Wooster, who read the manuscript with the discerning eyes of a former editor and who has given valuable support toward its completion.

Dr. Clayton S. Ellsworth, department of history, Dr. Donald MacKenzie, department of art, Dr. Charles B. Moke, department of geology. Dr. Atlee Stroup and Professor Verne C. Bechill, department of sociology, valued colleagues at the College of Wooster, who have assisted in countless details in their fields of specialty.

Raymond E. Dix, publisher of the *Wooster Daily Record*, for unfailing support through the years and for ready access to newspaper files.

Alma Kaufman, Wooster, staff reporter of the *Record*, whose own firsthand associations with the Amish have often been of service to the author and who has herself helped to dispel many untruths and half-truths about the Amish of Ohio.

Howard Yoder and Lester L. Litwiller, Wooster, long-time friends, for repeated advice.

Edna Kienzle Comin, Nancy Curry McSweeney, and Dorothy Seiler Walters, all of Wooster, for painstaking efforts in preparing the manuscript for the publisher.

Harold Thut, Orrville, Ohio, for introducing the author to the Oak Grove community.

The Reverend Virgil Gerig, Pandora, Ohio, former pastor of the Oak Grove Church, Smithville, who clarified many points of Mennonite life and doctrine during the writing of the manuscript.

Dr. Oliver D. Diller, Wooster, of the Ohio State Agricultural Experiment Station, for repeated trips through the roads and lanes of Amishland.

Ross L. Gerber, Smithville, Ohio, for suggestions about the Sugarcreek *Budget*.

George R. Smith, Sugarcreek, Ohio, publisher of the *Budget*, who answered countless questions about his unusual country newspaper.

Members of the East Union Amish districts who graciously allowed an outsider to share in their community life.

Grace Goulder (Mrs. Robert Izant), Hudson, Ohio, for urging completion of the book.

Dr. Harold S. Bender, Goshen, Indiana, dean, Goshen College, who as editor of the *Mennonite Quarterly Review* has made important suggestions about Mennonite historiography.

Preston Barba, Allentown, Pennsylvania, editor of the "Pennsylvanisch Deitsch Eck" in the *Allentown Morning Call*, who published early chapters of this book.

Dr. Alfred Louis Shoemaker, Lancaster, Pennsylvania, founder and editor of *Pennsylvania Folklife*.

Grant M. Stoltzfus, Harrisonburg, Virgina, professor at Eastern Mennonite College, for suggestions leading to deeper insights into the language of the *Ausbund*.

Aaron Esh, Bird-in-Hand, Pennsylvania, and O. J. Smith, Lancaster, Pennsylvania, for information about the printing of the *Ausbund*.

Ralph Ely, Barberton, Ohio, former superintendent, Wayne County public schools, for information pertaining to school problems.

Dr. Thomas A. Sebeok, University of Indiana, Bloomington, Indiana, and Dr. Wayland D. Hand, University of California at Los Angeles, of The American Folklore Society, for encouragement and publication of "Amish Wedding Days" in the *Journal of American Folklore*.

Dr. Tristam P. Coffin, Philadelphia, of the University of Pennsylvania, for the invitation to present the chapter on the Sugarcreek *Budget* before the American Folklore Society meeting in Philadelphia, December, 1960.

Dr. E. Heyse-Dummer, Illinois College, Jacksonville, Illinois, for the invitation to read selections before audiences of German teachers.

Dr. Adolph E. Schroeder, head, foreign language department, Kent State University, who invited the author to present his findings before graduate students participating in the National Defense Education Act language program.

Margaret Kate Moke, Wooster, former social worker in Wayne County, who gave assistance and information.

Helen Luckhardt Monnier, Chicago, devoted family friend, who read the manuscript from the viewpoint of a city observer.

Vilma Pikkoja, librarian, Holmes County Library, who invited the author to speak at the formal dedication of the Chestnut Ridge branch in the heart of Amishland.

Maudie L. Nesbitt, librarian of the College of Wooster and her staff, particularly Norine Flack, Ruth N. McClelland, and Sarah Painter, for their friendly assistance.

Deborah M. Chidester, Wooster, for the gift to the author of first editions of Mennonite literature.

Mrs. Joseph W. Yoder and the Yoder Publishing Company, Huntingdon, Pennsylvania, for permission to reproduce some examples of Amish *lieder* from the *Amish Hymn Book* by Joseph W. Yoder.

Finally, I wish to thank Sybil Gould, colleague in the College of Wooster, whose skilful pencil and sensitive nature have combined to capture the spirit and character of our Amish neighbors.

CONTENTS

xi

How very much I have again learned to love that class of people one calls the lowly, but which, God knows, is certainly the highest! All virtues are gathered in them, simple-mindedness, modesty, straightforwardness, faithfulness, joy over little things in life, harmlessness, patience—patience—perseverance—I do not want to lose myself in exclamations.

GOETHE IN LETTER
TO FRAU VON STEIN, GOSLAR
DECEMBER 4, 1777

INTRODUCTION

A DAY WITH THE AMISH

It was early on a beautiful Sunday morning in July, off U.S. Highway 250, southeast of Wooster, beyond the village of Apple Creek. Traces of buggy wheels from a county lane showed on the gravel road washed clean by the thunderstorms of the night before. Other tracks entered the same road from other lanes. A crossroad brought still more. Down the road the tracks became more pronounced. Now there must have been fifty to sixty of them. All seemed to converge on a narrow side road. The meeting place must be close by now. Yes, there across the ripening wheat field, several hundred feet from the road, much activity was in evidence. Men in dark blue trousers and coats with hooks and eyes instead of buttons and without collars or sleeves, with big broad black hats, and with white shirt sleeves and here and there blue ones, were busy unharnessing their well-groomed horses from the black-topped buggies. The light, high-wheeled carriages were arranged in orderly fashion within the farmyard. There was no mistaking it; here was the meeting place of a "Gemei of Amishleut," one of some forty-two districts[1] of Amish neighbors in this section of east-central Ohio.

I left my car in the lane, because nothing so characteristic of the twentieth century should spoil a gathering of apostolic Christianity in a semi-medieval setting. The host of the day, a young Amishman, was bustling about, busy with the care of guests and horses. Since no one objected to my presence at the religious service, I walked toward a huge building, resembling a Swiss barn, where sliding doors stood open. Sounds of singing echoed from the emptied, tidied middle section of the upper floor. Eight rows of plain wooden benches filled the threshing den. On the right, grandmothers, mothers, and their small daughters had taken their seats. In one row I counted eighteen adults and ten young girls. Their dresses fell in long folds from a high neckline down to the ankles, presenting, apart from the black, all the shades of purple, blue, and green. Over these the women wore full-length white gauze-like aprons. On some this apron was belted at the waist; on others the two halves of the upper part of the apron crossed the chest. All the aprons were tucked in at the neck and then fell in the back in a V shape down to the waist, where the tip disappeared in a narrow belt. Each woman's hair was parted in the middle, combed smoothly aside, and rolled under a fine net prayer cap. This was tied under the chin with a thin ribbon. Children and married women wore white caps and the unmarried wore black. Even the tiniest toddlers resembled their elders, except that their aprons were buttoned in the back.

On the opposite side, facing the women, sat the men. They seemed to cluster mainly around a table in the far corner where the song leader held forth. Their hats were off, laid beneath the benches or in the straw. Seeing these men I thought of the Seven Dwarfs, surely their prototypes, but there were seven times as many. All the older men had

[1] Because they do not associate with the other Old Order Gemei, this number does not include the Swartzentruber, King, and Stutzman districts.

beards, and of what imposing variety they were! Some were white and pointed, others were black, brown, red, of all shapes and lengths. The men, however, were cleanly shaven around the mouth, with smooth cheeks as well. The hair on each head was patted down from the crown to the sides and trimmed over the ears and neck.

There were still a few vacant seats when I took my place on the back row. No face showed suspicion, and all had an expression of peace. I saw on each face contentment, frugality, integrity, simplicity, the absence of dissipation, and the marks of hard work. Cosmetics neither concealed nor accentuated an emotion on these faces. These people were much more concerned with the singing of their century-old hymns that told of the faith and suffering of martyrs than with a modern visitor. The melody was sung without harmony or accompaniment. Its near falsetto pitch almost hurt my ears. During a pause between songs, the bishop, two preachers, and the deacon, who handles the affairs of the poor, entered, shaking hands on the right and left and proceeding all the way to the far side of the barn. Then the oldest man, with a flowing white beard, whom I judged to be in his seventies, preached for forty minutes: "All those who thirst for righteousness shall see the Lord Jesus when he comes, but not in the flesh but in the spirit." His speech was fluent "Pennsylvania German" dialect. He spoke without notes, outline, or manuscript and with a constant movement of either arm or hand. His address was furnished with abundant scriptural references. I thought I saw the Apostle John himself expounding on the life of the Lord on earth. The chaff-flecked barn door served as a backdrop. The people and the scene produced the sense that primitive Christianity had come back to earth again with the disciples bringing the good tidings. The twittering of many sparrows, a pair of doves in the high rafters of the barn, and the stamping of the fly-bitten horses on the floor below added to the primitive atmosphere. The whole assembly knelt in silent prayer on the rough barn floor. By this time

3

there were more than 150 people in the barn. The younger boys overflowed behind the men onto the straw. When the bishop began to read from the New Testament with the inflection of a Gregorian chant, everyone stood in reverent attention. The text was long. The preacher of the next sermon was a younger man, of large stature and florid complexion, with a full, dark brown beard. His forehead resembled a halo in contrast with his well-tanned face. His theme was "Who believeth and is baptized, shall be saved." He enlarged on this message for seventy minutes. He was particularly anxious to exhort the younger men and women to commit themselves to the Amish faith and be baptized—an outward evidence of their adherence to the Anabaptist beliefs of their fathers.

Four confessions of faith followed. One was spirited and lasted about ten minutes, whereupon one of the preachers made a long prayer while everyone knelt. The boys on the straw turned over on their stomachs as evidence of their devotion. The blessing, however, was received by all adults while they stood with bowed heads. A few announcements and a hymn concluded the meeting. By this time it was far beyond one o'clock. Indeed it was remarkable that with neither solos nor musical interludes, no collections, and no responsive readings, the congregation remained silent during the entire time in a devout and attentive attitude, no one paying attention to his opposite or neighbor. True, older boys left to do chores below in the stable and babies whined or cried as time dragged for them.

Upon conclusion of the meeting the men arose; the women remained seated. The barn doors were opened wide, and the men left first, followed by the women, who moved toward the farmhouse to prepare the communal meal. The men visited with each other and with the visitor from modern Wooster. There was friendliness and cordiality in the handshake of these men of the "left wing of the Reformation." The visitor was told how in 1521 their forefathers in Zurich had tried to separate church and state and reintro-

4

duce on a verbal biblical basis apostolic times with baptism of the adults, but had paid a price in persecution and blood as no other Protestant sect. Again in 1693 "laxity in discipline" had caused the preacher Jakob Ammann to take his flock away and thus to preserve the hard-fought victory against encroaching changes. From Jakob Ammann came the name "Amish." At last America had given them a haven of refuge and here, without fear, they could worship and work and live as they deemed best.

The farmhouse, of course, was too small to serve all at one sitting. Boards laid across two church benches and covered with white linen cloth made the dining table. It was heavily loaded to say the least. For every four persons there was a big bowl of thickly creamed pudding; everyone helped himself with his large soup spoon, according to the principle that nothing is unclean to the undefiled. Each reached with a knife for bread, good country butter, and the sweets and sours that were provided abundantly. A gray-bearded, healthy and prosperous-looking farmer led the procession to the table. On my right was a tall, middle-aged, dark man, with a straggly beard and hair and flashing black eyes. When our row was filled, an equal number of women moved to opposite seats. I saw some smaller children, neat and attractive and as contented and well behaved as any I have ever seen. When all were seated, my older host folded his hands and bowed his head in silent prayer. Eating seemed all-important, and no words were exchanged across the table. An elderly woman replenished the food on the table. When everyone had eaten, all bowed their heads again in silent prayer, and then the men left the room; the women did not rise until the men had left.

I met the bishop, the spiritual ruler of the congregation, who marries, baptizes, and buries members of the Amish community. He, too, was of the soil, as were all his brethren. He had never attended high school, college, or seminary, but was chosen from among the preachers for his deeper knowledge of men and his rich spiritual resources.

He received no salary inasmuch as the things of the spirit cannot be repaid with earthly means. I had to admire the man, small in stature, not unlike Paul, with full broad titian-red beard and long flowing hair. His eyes were so clear, peaceful, and kind, yet intelligent and alert, and his expression was so tender that it must have been the result of long periods of prayer and meditation. At once he could be recognized as the true shepherd of his flock. He accompanied me through the farmyard to the gate. There he shook hands silently with the men and the women whom he had not met before. Everyone stood and looked at him as at a trusted friend and father. He was happy that I had remained for the entire service, and he hoped that his congregation had not given me cause to be disturbed.

The latest discoveries of science and the most recent inventions of electricity, tractor, and automobile have not penetrated the lives of the Amish; nevertheless, the restless, curious, and acquisitive advocate of gadgets of fashion, mechanics, and science may find here a healthy antidote. American civilization has here one of its most stable and self-sufficient elements. I could leave then with no other thought than that a few hours spent with the Old Order Amish was like a retreat into life in the past, a welcome halt to the feverish progress of the present.

This was my first formal association with the Old Order Amish. The occasion is repeated Sunday after Sunday throughout this section of Ohio, and yet it remains unknown to most local citizens, rushing by in their swift automobiles. The Amish have extended to me the courtesy of observing them at close range because they do not consider me an intruder. I speak their language and their dialect. They find me interesting as a German teacher, in my manner of speaking, in my curiosity and concern for them. I can tell them of the old homeland from which we both have come and which they will probably never see. When they do leave their farms and homesteads, their habits seem strange to urban and suburban Americans. These do not seem so peculiar to me because I see in them "old country" ways preserved in the midst of the New World. On the other hand, I too have come from abroad, with ancestors not far removed from country living. And yet while it has been my endeavor to become part of the life and fabric of America, these people exhibit the contrary ambition. They want to uphold the heritage of their ancestors uncluttered by modern devices or distorted by current educational theories. To me, a German-born American, the Amish now seem more German than the peasants of my native land.

My profession called me to the College of Wooster, Wooster, Wayne County, Ohio, in 1937. Although my first concern is to impart German language and literature to young minds, I have found here a second interest. The Amish whetted my curiosity about the early history of this Ohio community. How was it settled? Why did these people come here? What is their background? Who inspired them? How do they live today? These and countless other questions could not be answered primarily from books or by sitting in an office. My queries drove me across unfamiliar country roads and rutted lanes, to the homes of bishops, deacons, farmers. The following pages show my findings. The Amish have come to regard me as their friend, and they are for me my neighbors.

CHAPTER I

THE AMISH IN A NEW LAND

SETTLING THE OHIO FRONTIER

They view'd the country, found it rich in wood,
Discover'd goodly springs, and felt as they
Were in their own dear native land once more.
Then they resolved to settle on the spot;
Erected there the ancient town of Schwytz;
And many a day of toil had they to clear
The tangled brake and forest's spreading roots.
Meanwhile their numbers grew, the soil became
Unequal to sustain them. . . .
Yet ever mindful of their parent stem,
The men of Schwytz, from all the stranger race,
That since that time have settled in the land,
Each other recognize. Their hearts still know,
And beat fraternally to kindred blood
                    [H. H. Boyesen's translation].

The settling of Wayne County, Ohio, bears striking similarity to this description of the occupation of the Forest
Cantons of Switzerland as given by Stauffacher in the fa-

9

mous Rutli scene in *William Tell*. Indeed, Schiller wrote these lines about the same time that the first native Germans, the first Pennsylvania Germans, Swiss, and followers of Menno Simons arrived in the east-central section of Ohio. The influx of the "Dutch," as these various German-speaking groups were called, was so pronounced that in 1875 they were estimated to comprise better than three-fourths of the population of the county.

Wayne County, once a vast expanse of wilderness including a large part of what is now Ohio, Indiana, Illinois, Wisconsin, and all of Michigan, was the sixth county of the great Northwest Territory defined by the Ordinance of 1787. After the formation of the state of Ohio in 1803, with accompanying boundaries and political subdivisions, Wayne County was twice restricted in size. In 1846 it was reduced to its present 551 square miles contained within rectangular lines of demarcation. Flowing waters and immense glaciers long ago left their mark upon the landscape. The rolling countryside with its gentle hills and alluvial plains still contains large swamps and lakes. Located on the southern declivity of the dividing ridge between the Great Lakes region and the Ohio and Mississippi Basin, this area has become one of the most agriculturally productive of the eighty-eight counties in the state. A crop failure caused by unfavorable weather is unknown, and the men working here have used both soil and climate to best advantage.

Particularly rich in egg and poultry products, Wayne County is eminent also for its dairy industry, the number and value of cattle and all livestock, production of hay, amount of feed purchased, and the use of fertilizer and lime. In the raising of potatoes it ranks first in the state, and its wheat production is high. Added to natural fertility are the economic advantages of a location near the great centers of Ohio's industrial and metropolitan wealth. Some of the state's largest cities are within easy reach of Wooster, the county seat. Columbus, the state capital, is 90 miles southwest, Mansfield 30 miles west, Cleveland 50 miles

north, Akron 25 miles and Youngstown 70 miles northeast, Massillon 20 miles and Canton 30 miles east.

The Ordinance of 1787, passed by the Congress of the newborn American nation to establish the government of the Northwest Territory, decreed:

> There shall be neither slavery nor involuntary servitude in the said territory otherwise than in the punishment of crimes, whereof the party shall have been duly convicted: provided always, that any person escaping into the same from labor and service is lawfully claimed in any one of the original states, such fugitives may be lawfully reclaimed, and conveyed to the person claiming his or her labor or service aforesaid.[1]

The decree that "neither slavery nor involuntary servitude" was to prevail in the newly opened lands bounded by the Ohio River on one end and the Great Lakes on the other could not help attracting the attention of freedom-loving people. A veritable flood of emigrants from all parts of the Atlantic seaboard and many also from foreign lands crowded into this area. "Made of such ingredients," wrote Caleb Atwater, the earliest historian of Ohio, "it is easy to conceive, that with the addition of the young, the enterprising, athletic, bold, daring and ambitious, of all states and all countries, the whole mass would be such as never was found anywhere else in the world."[2] The population of the state increased from a bare 3,000 in 1791 to 230,760 in 1810, and it was just short of a million by 1830.

The settling of the state occurred generally along three lines: pioneers from New England occupied the northern region along Lake Erie and the western part of the state and the region around Marietta; those from Virginia and Carolina moved into the southern counties along the Ohio River; comparatively late came the Pennsylvanians and foreigners who claimed the middle belt and certain border towns in the south and north.

The counties located in the forbidding interior wilder-

11

ness were only slowly opened. Contemporaries even called the dismal region the "dark and bloody ground." The Indian did not easily surrender his accessible food supply or his freedom of movement to an invader, friendly and peaceable enough at first, who soon proved himself aggressive and restrictive. Successful uprisings against General Josiah Harmar and Governor Arthur St. Clair foreboded ill for any white settler. "Mad" Anthony Wayne deserves the credit for clearing the way for central Ohio's rapid development. In August, 1794, he won a decisive victory over the organized hordes of Indians at the Battle of Fallen Timbers. The following year the Indians signed a treaty with the white man, ceding much of the land they had called their own to their former enemies. Only isolated and local attacks remained to be feared after this. Nevertheless the territory was only slowly settled and became known as the "school of heroism." It brought forth its share of adventurous men from the Atlantic Coast, and the difficulty of its settling added to its glory.

The dense forests of the "backbone counties" of Stark, Wayne, Ashland, and Richland were too threatening for the first adventurers to the new frontier. When statehood was granted to Ohio, there was as yet not a single white man in the large tract of land which is now Wayne County. The earliest isolated squatter is believed to have lived there in 1806; three homesteads are known to have been built in the following year. So slow was the development at first that the second official Ohio census, of 1810, gives no indication of any settlement within the county of even 250 inhabitants. Only after the internecine warfare and rivalry between red man and white settler began finally to abate with the successful conclusion of the War of 1812 could the land be peacefully claimed. By 1825 every section of the county had been staked, and sixteen townships had been established, each with its own administration.

The settlers' interests were entirely centered upon the full cultivation and exploitation of their new forest home.

The men engaged in this venture, in the words of their contemporary Ben Douglass, were not and could not be

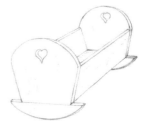

> an association of coach trimmers, guilders, carvers, peruckmakers and friseurs, but a thrifty, iron-clad, metalfisted legion of laborers; a brain-born irresistible army of thinkers and workers; a sweeping, slashing myriad of forest breakers and cordwood artisans, modelling out of the rude elements the thousand-aisled temple of civilization. . . . Men were not artificial figures, brainless swells, votaries of every gewgaw and bauble of fashion or folly. Women were not painted puppets, varnished inanities, enameled statuary, stuffed skeletons, dainty toys, and sickly butterflies.[3]

The influx of settlers into Wayne County was swift and steady after 1812. Many of the eastern states sent men and women versed in the ways of pioneering and democracy. Pennsylvania gave the largest share, with hardly a Keystone county being unrepresented in the records of early settlement. Some came from abroad, settled in Pennsylvania first, and then moved farther west. Indeed, so many Pennsylvanians of German origin came to Wayne County that any other place of origin was cause for comment. The biography of James Douglass, whose name could have spoken for itself, expressly states: "Although a native of Pennsylvania he was of Scotch-Irish parentage."[4] A typical example of the migratory pattern is Frederick Galehouse (ancestor of the family which produced the baseball player, Denny Galehouse) who was born in Baden, Germany, in 1781, was brought to Cumberland County, Pennsylvania, in 1786, and was one of the first white men in Wayne County after 1806.

Many settlers were free men for whom the East was too densely populated and land too scarce and expensive. Others had been indentured servants who took advantage of the West when they had served their time. The ancestor of a now prominent Wooster family had left Hamburg early in

13

the 1700's and was indentured for seven years. During his period of servitude he made three unsuccessful attempts to escape. When at last he crossed the Allegheny Mountains to stop in Fayette County, he had six children, two of whom were carried in wallets, or saddlebags, on horseback. One of his grandsons brought the family name into Wayne County and was among the first of its settlers. Similar is the case of Philip Brown, who, as an orphan at the age of fourteen, was bound out for seven years as an apprentice blacksmith in Somerset County. He became the first German Baptist preacher in Wayne County.

The trek to the new claim in the forest was a trial, with the last part the most hazardous and arduous. Many are the accounts of the difficult exodus of the pioneer from his eastern home, but the vicissitudes encountered upon arrival were even greater. In the eastern states, roads, taverns, and co-travelers often added to the comfort of the journey; with the approach of the Ohio River each emigrant was on his own. Sometimes members of a family or a group of friends or neighbors banded together, but just as often adventure westward was an individual or at most a one-family undertaking. The records also tell of well-established fathers in Pennsylvania who left home to help their sons get started in the Ohio wilderness. One Harry Lash, for example, drove his son in a wagon with tools and furnishings, built a log cabin 18 by 18 feet, and then left the son with five dollars in cash. In spite of clearing ten acres of land, however, the son was unable to raise the necessary two dollars and fifty cents within the first year, and the father had to come again to aid his boy. At times one member of a family tried staking a claim and then invited relatives to come and look for suitable locations while enjoying his hospitality. Thus a Valentine Ault from York and Washington counties visited an uncle in Wayne County but spent the first night in the new land in a tree and "stayed on it all night" because of the many wolves.

Game was plentiful and formed the chief food, but do-

14

mestic animals were extremely difficult to raise in the wild surroundings. Even when sheep and hogs were kept close to the homestead and watched over by dogs they became easy victims of wolves and bears. Michael Totten lost eleven of his flock of twelve sheep in one winter's night. As late as 1824–25 the pioneers of neighboring Summit County (Akron) to the east held several "drives" against the marauders. One of them resulted in the killing of twenty-six bears.

At first the homesteader followed the Indian trails and had to cut a road through the woods to reach his claim with his ox- or horse-drawn wagon. Often it was safer to walk than to ride, because of the rocking and shaking of the vehicle. If there were women, they had to help in the labor. Naturally, some young men came alone at first, built a cabin on their new land, and then returned after a year or two to fetch the family or to acquire a wife. The German brothers, John and Reuben Newkirk, proceeded in this way in 1814. When the newly wedded couples came back into the neighborhood of their claims, however, they found one of the streams so swollen that further passage seemed impossible. At last the men decided to swim across with the horses. Vines were tied from the horses to the wagons on the other side, and possessions were pulled over the water. Jakob Planck, a miller by trade whose flour was the pride of the early inhabitants of Wayne County, came to prepare a home and then went back in 1821 to Mifflin County, Pennsylvania, to fetch his wife and eleven children.

An added difficulty for the earliest settlers was the absence of markets and the lack of money. Wheat and corn were cheap because there was an abundant harvest and no available market. On the other hand, every other article for home and farm was extremely dear because commerce was practically non-existent. Most of the clothing was homespun, and every family was proficient in supplying itself. Salt and coffee were precious commodities; the latter was used only on special family celebrations, a baptism, birthday, or wedding. Some of the pioneers drove to market in Cleveland, some fifty miles to the north, others preferred Canton, some thirty miles to the east. It is reported that in 1816 a whole bushel of wheat would pay for one pound of coffee. At this date a barrel of salt cost fifteen dollars, salt also being used as a medium of exchange. One Wayne County farmer bought a two-horse wagon with two barrels of salt; one large farm at this time sold for a hundred gallons of corn whisky. Cash money was a rarity.

Whatever the motives and incentives for leaving the native land, on the newly opened frontier each claimant had an opportunity to acquire real property and to live according to the dictates of his own conscience. Here the immigrant from abroad and the American from the eastern seaboard had the same rights and privileges of holding land, of obtaining solid, free-hold property rights to the best and cheapest land west of the Alleghenies.

Concerning the immigration of the German-speaking peoples, there are certain noticeable contrasts between the Central Europe of that day and Ohio of the Northwest Territory. On the other side of the Atlantic the French Revolution had promised freedom and had raised the hopes of many people. At the same time the constant threat of religious intolerance, nuisance laws, and arbitrary feudal lords, the havoc and devastation of the Napoleonic wars, accompanied by crop failures and finally by social and political upheaval and oppression, drove men of deep religious conviction and lovers of freedom to this "new land." With the threats of Indian warfare and attacks by wild beasts removed, the great inundation of the country began. There is therefore a parallel between the settling of Ohio and the emigration from Germany: the increase in the population of the state reached its greatest stride about the middle of the century, at which time the flight from politically shaken Europe was at its height.

The German-speaking Mennonites were the largest single group to settle in central Ohio and these people today still form the largest outstanding ethnic and religious community within the state. It is easy to see why they should have chosen this area. They found a landscape with hills and dales not unlike those of their native land, and they discovered a soil which they knew from long experience to be suitable for their sort of life and purpose. Abundant, clear springs and hardwood trees—oak, maple, hickory, and walnut—were to them unmistakable tokens of rich fertility and signs of future reward. Their whole past history of persecution and wandering had made them keen to the indexes with which nature reveals its inner secrets. After all, these men of toil were not looking for quick riches but mainly for a haven; they wanted not rest and ease, only respite from the interference of men. These seemed to exist here. Their past experience had steeled them for hard labor, and work in the wilderness was lightened because it was strictly for themselves. They chose well, and their claims are a credit to their acumen and energy.

The main Pennsylvania Mennonite line was Old Order Amish. Their settlement began in 1807 when a party under the leadership of Jakob (Jockle) Miller was sent from Somerset County to scout for new land. From Pittsburgh the party went down the Ohio River and up the Mississippi to Iowa. However the men could not reach a decision as to where to stake a claim. On their return trip, made overland, they passed through the Killbuck Valley. Here they had no doubts. This was the new land for them. In a few years the settlement grew and spread; today it is the most extensive Amish settlement in America. Many very large families came to the area, and the many identical names which have resulted are now so confusing that elaborate sets of middle initials and nicknames are used. The story is told of a doctor who called to attend a Schlabach family, traveled all night to find it, and finally gave up hope of finding the Schlabachs who needed him among the scores of Schlabachs in the area.

Several genealogies of original Ohio Amish families are

now available. For instance, the family tree of Jeremiah Miller, who as the seventh child among twelve was brought into Ohio in 1819 at the age of two, had 261 descendants in 1943. A younger brother Joni Miller, born in 1824, has a progeny of 550 descendants. Their grandfather Samuel Mueller had arrived on the ship "Chance" in Philadelphia on November 1, 1763, with 192 other passengers from the canton of Berne, Switzerland.

The largest group of Mennonite immigrants coming directly from abroad was heralded by Benedict Schraag (Schrock) who settled in Green Township, the most fertile section of Wayne County, just northeast of Wooster. It is not surprising that he sent letters full of praise to the brethren left behind. Soon they followed. The good news spread throughout the Emmenthal region, Canton Berne, Switzerland, and north into the Jura mountains, to Alsace and the Palatinate. A famine during the years 1816–17 following the hardships of the War of Liberation impelled the majority of the Sonnenberg congregation of the Jura and many from Alsace to emigrate. Isaac Sommer, David Kirchhofer, Peter and Ulrich Lehmann, with their families, were the first to follow. Then the flood began which eventually filled the county and only abated in 1837. By then, Sonnenberg, Chester, Chippewa, and other communities had been founded, and little land remained. Now some settlers began to look for cheaper land and wider spaces farther west, and Mennonite settlement flowed over into western Ohio, Indiana, and Illinois. The new leader was Michael Neuenschwander. Born in 1778 in the Alsace, he left his native home for America on May 15, 1823. In fifteen days he reached Paris; by June 5, he was in Le Havre. His fifth child was born on the ship "Eolus" on June 11. After forty-three sailing days he arrived safely at New London, Connecticut. His itinerary took him to New York, Amboy, Easton, Bethlehem, Reading, Harrisburg, Bedford, Greensburg, and Pittsburgh. Here one of his children died. After a week he resumed his journey to Beavertown, then to Canton, Ohio,

18

and finally he reached little Chippewa Creek, Green Township, on October 5, 1823. The entire trip had taken nearly six months. Some of his descendants remained in the Canton area; the name of Neuenschwander is still alive in the region. Others who moved farther with him returned later under the name of Neiswander.

David Houmard has left different details of his journey. His trip from Canton Berne, Switzerland, took seventeen weeks and one day. He brought wife, father and mother, and an outfit of baggage, including a wagon, which weighed about 1,765 pounds. He came up the Hudson River to Albany, was one of the first foreigners to sail the Erie Canal, and then took a boat to Cleveland, Ohio. There he bought a yoke of oxen for $36.00 and drove to his destination in Wayne County.

It is worthy of note that in this section of Ohio alone there are more Mennonites now than in Switzerland, the original home. A detailed picture of these thrifty religious pioneers who helped transform a forest wilderness into a leading Ohio county is recorded in the succeeding pages.

Mennonite Divisions

The Mennonite community in the east-central counties of Ohio, particularly Wayne, Holmes, Tuscarawas, and Coshocton, is the largest and most compact of its kind in America. Distributed over a large farming area with a diversity of scenery, the followers of Menno Simons have had to adapt not only to changes in land contours but also to the surrounding American culture. The variety of religious experience and expression that has resulted is as remarkable as the transition from level to hilly land or the difference between the modern city and a hinterland farmyard. While the same confession of faith serves as guide to life and salvation for the Mennonite living within the city and for his rural brother, the Central Conference Mennonite stands to the Old Order Amish as the twentieth-century Christian to

the Franciscan friar. The fact remains that these extremes, as well as the several intermediary positions, all take their origins from one fundamentalist, conservative root. Off-shoots of the various Mennonite persuasions have, in general, flourished and grown, although some have vanished completely. Only the Old Order Amish sect, however, has so increased within the last 150 years as to include some forty-two districts. The growth, increase, and expansion of Mennonitism, in various shapes, has not yet been halted. New concentration upon hard-core fundamentalism is being matched by wider acculturation on the periphery.

In 1838 when Caleb Atwater wrote the first history of the state,[5] the Mennonites had not made enough impression to receive mention among the thirty-two religious bodies he described. If Atwater was aware of the Mennonites at all, he must have included them among the large group he called the "Separatists." Nevertheless, the Mennonites were firmly established at that date in many parts of the state. Later, in 1848, in H. Howe's *Historical Collections of Ohio*, they again found no place. Howe mentions, however, an extensive settlement in the eastern part of Holmes County of "Dunkards who originated from Eastern Pennsylvania and speak the German language." He goes on to say that the Dunkards are "excellent farmers [who] live in good substantial style." The men he describes as wearing long beards and shad-bellied coats, using hooks and eyes instead of buttons. "The females are attired in petticoats and short gowns, caps without frills, and when doing outdoor labor, instead of bonnets, wear broad-brimmed hats."[6] In fact, this description applied not only to the Dunkards, or Brethren as they are often called, but to all the Mennonites of the old orders and would be accurate today.

Howe was not totally unaware of the Amish within the state. In connection with Putnam County he writes:

> In Riley is a settlement of "Aymish or Omish," a sect of the "Mennonites or Harmless Christians."

They derive their name from Aymen their founder, and were originally known as Aymenites. This sect wear long beards, and reject all superfluities in dress, diet and property. They have ever been remarkable for industry, frugality, temperance and simplicity. At an early day many of the Omish emigrated from Germany to Pennsylvania. When they first came to the country they had neither churches nor grave-yards. "A Church," said they, "we do not require, for in the depth of the thicket, in the forest, on the water, in the field and in the dwelling, God is always present." Many of their descendants, deviating from the practice of their forefathers, have churches and burial grounds.[7]

In Wayne County's first comprehensive history, written in 1878, the Mennonites again are not listed, although most of the eastern part of the county was theirs. Only the "Swiss" of the Sonnenberg congregation are mentioned by Ben Douglass. For him the members of this congregation are

> mostly farmers and very industrious; are good horse traders and revel in the effluvia of decomposed cheese. The older ones robustly oppose the introduction of books, incline to antagonize education, and indulge in habits wholly un-American. They introduced the painting of doghouses and the manufacture of applejack in Sugar Creek township.[8]

Interestingly enough the "Swiss" are here not only recognized for the first time but are already in conflict with a believer in the scientific spirit, then beginning to pervade America, and the progressive is not complimentary in his references to them.

Douglass calls the settlers of the Sonnenberg district Mennonite but states that "they did not pretend to know what their peculiar tenets were, and even their members seemed ignorant of their history and gave no very intelligent idea of their faith." Again the author calls attention to the fact that they are mostly farmers and that "some of them are in horse trading and are fair judges of equine flesh and can drive a bargain with skill and acumen. The manufacture of cheese is one of their industries and accomplishments, from which they derive considerable profit."[9] The description is undoubtedly true, for bargaining is still one of the chief Mennonite avocations; regular weekly auctions held in their territory are crowded with participants. And the Mennonite section of Ohio has become the center of Swiss cheese manufacture and ranks first in Ohio's dairy industry.

Later still, Bowen, in A History of Wayne County, Ohio,[10] acknowledges the Sonnenberg settlement. In organization it was then in no way different from the present Amish "Gemei," but he notes that

> the Modern Mennonite as a rule does not pretend to know just what the history of his sect is, or just what he now believes. He knows they are opposed to war and going to law. They follow farm life, as a rule, and are very industrious . . . and . . . in 1820 organized a church. [In the past in Switzerland] they were compelled to flee to the mountains, where they were not allowed to live in towns or own land, and were forced to farm wild mountain lands and pay high rent for the same.[11]

The Sonnenberg congregation referred to by both Douglass and Bowen worshiped in private dwellings until 1834, when the first church was built. The congregation is still in existence, but its present practices are unlike the old forms. After many schisms over externals, which the original group stoutly rejected up to World War II, it, too, went modern.

Over the years in Ohio, members of the faith have left both the rural environment and church affiliation. A noteworthy example is Mrs. Otelia Augsburger Compton, mother of the noted educators and scientists, whose father was an Alsatian Mennonite immigrant. When Mrs. Compton came to live in the city of Wooster, she joined the Presbyterian church and eventually deposed her hood and bonnet. On the other hand, a Mennonite mission founded within the city of Wooster in 1942 to evangelize non-church people has become since 1951 a substantial local congregation with its own brick sanctuary and fellowship rooms. The practical result of this "mission" has been that men and women crowded out of agricultural occupations found in it a renewed bond with their original faith. Wayne County offers, therefore, one of the best instances of what happens to a conservative European Protestant sect when it has found a haven of unrestricted development and unmolested existence.

The freedom from all outside restrictions and the novelty of adjusting to American culture have had, and are continuing to have, a disturbing and disruptive influence upon the conservative Mennonite. In Europe he had learned to adapt himself to generations of masters, to exploitation and suppression, to ecclesiastical and governmental proscriptions. He had opposed these hardships with unity and solidarity in faith and practice. However in America something unaccustomed engulfed him. If his reaction to the surrounding world had, by necessity and by faith, been negative and if he had exercised his greatest strength in this negative opposition, with the release of restrictive inhibitions his reasons for united resistance were diminished. In the New World no one encroached upon his life, activity, or religion. Slowly he came to realize that positive living, the exhilaration of an optimistic world view, and expanding opportunity were for him as they were for his neighbor. What to make of these liberties, how to cope with the chances available were distracting and baffling problems. Between the extremes of faithful preservation and complete overthrow of the inherited past are varieties of interpretation and adaptations which somehow seem more pronounced and characteristic than do those of any other church.

The presence of diverse branches of the Mennonite faith exhibiting the greatest possible variety of religious accommodation and cultural acclimatization make Wayne County doubly attractive to the student. It is most unusual that within the narrowly defined limits of one Ohio county such a perplexity of branches of one faith could arise. These often contradictory forms of interpretation range from the severe fundamentalism of the pioneer stem to a Mennonitism which remains so, apparently, in name only. Another group, which refuses to be identified as Mennonite, retains many of the cult and behavior practices of the Mennonites.

As indicated in the preceding chapter, the members of the faith chose the site of their future home very carefully. The topography of the land and the productivity of the soil counted heavily in its favor. But none of the founding groups calculated the effects of the progress of the surrounding culture. As it has turned out, the varieties farthest removed from direct lines of communication with the "world" have been able to preserve themselves better in their old accustomed ways than those on the fringes.

The Mennonite settlements border on and extend northward from the deep, eroded valleys and narrow ridges of the unglaciated part of adjacent Holmes County. Such extremes of physiographical relief have always been avoided by men born to the soil. Yet in the hilly country there is a safeguard to the mores of the Old Order Amish people. Lines of communication are fewer, the region generally is less accessible, off the "beaten path." The congregations which are farthest removed from the city live, therefore, in relative seclusion and have less trouble in keeping the faithful pure and uncontaminated by modern modes and manners. In contrast, the more liberal groups, such as the Beachy Amish, have allowed cars and telephones, though not radios and television, and the so-called "Conservative Amish" or Church Amish have even built houses of worship along the two federal roads which traverse the region, U.S. Highways 30 and 62.

The "Swiss" Mennonites live in relatively undulating landscape not unlike that of central Switzerland. These "Swiss" of the Sonnenberg congregation have in the past preferred to live a totally isolated existence. Old Order Mennonites then form a transition to less restrictive groups of Amish Mennonites and Mennonites to the north. The conservative elements begin to disappear between U.S. Highway 250, which runs southeasterly from the city of Wooster and U.S. Highway 30, Lincoln Highway, which bisects the county into northern and southern halves. North of the Lincoln Highway in more-and-more level country crossed by the Wooster-Akron highway and the main lines of the Pennsylvania, the Baltimore and Ohio, and the Erie railroads, the most liberal Mennonites have established their homes. The best farming land is found in these level regions of the northern townships of Wayne County where the divide between the Ohio and Mississippi Basin and the Great Lakes region is reached. This fertile landscape, gradually leveling northward, is accompanied by a more liberal adaptation to present-day America. As the soil becomes more productive, so the Mennonite farmer tends to use more modern agricultural implements; his religious practices, his religious outlook upon life, is broader and his faith and life are less rigid and more related to customary Protestant practice.

It is possible to distinguish at least twelve separate groups of Mennonites in Wayne County, according to their affiliation with or independence from national religious conferences. While it is not always easy to differentiate between one and another of the middle groups, there is an unmistakable cleavage between extremes. Practically all Mennonites use the Dortrecht Confession of Faith of 1632. The distinguishing marks, however, between one group and another are in the interpretation of the cardinal doctrines, the practical application of the rules of faith, and the customs that have become associated with these doctrines. From south to north, from hills to plains, from con-

servativism to liberalism, from rejection of, to adaptation to, American culture patterns, these are the main groups:

>Old Order Amish or House Amish
>Beachy Amish
>"Conservative Amish" or Church Amish
>"Swiss" Mennonites
>Church of God in Christ
>Old Mennonites
>Old Order Wisler Mennonites
>Mennonites
>Middle District Conference, General Conference
>"New Amish," Apostolic Christian
>Reformed Mennonites
>Oak Grove Mennonites

The nomenclature can only be momentarily accurate, one must admit, because new alignments are constantly developing, and the researcher who tries to classify and bring order to the various groups is of necessity immediately outdated. For instance, in the very first group, the Old Order Amish, there exist now the larger Swartzentruber and the smaller Stutzman and King offshoots which differ about certain external minutiae such as the cut of hair, the size of the brim of the hat, or the use of a glass window in the side of the buggy. Yet these items of differentiation are considered matters of salvation itself—and association with people who have not accepted them is forbidden.

There is also a wide difference in behavior patterns among the General Conference Mennonites to which the Middle District belongs. This latter Wayne County group had always been regarded as the most progressive of all followers of the faith, but, within the past few years, they have been joined with people with whom they have very little in common except the Confession of Faith. One perceives similar differentiations within the "Swiss" and the Old Order Wisler Mennonites.

One recognizes Mennonite congregations and identifies

them by the degree of acclimatization and adjustment which each group has allowed itself. Congregations other than the Old Order Amish constantly find themselves confronted with new problems which demand a re-examination and justification of their position. The relative strength or weakness of response toward the enticement of the "world," the "times," the "city," or the surrounding culture have produced the varied groupings within the county. If the answer is negative, it is often only a temporary one. A dubious compromise is at times reached by allowing, for instance, a musical instrument in the home or to the children, but not in the place of worship. With that, however, the door is opened; gradually general acceptance is acknowledged.

The cause of schism, dissension, or separation is often such a tangible item as a wedding ring, a pair of spectacles, a necktie, rubber suspenders, leather belts, barber haircuts, or a lady's hair style. If a woman chooses to wear a wedding ring, it may become the center of a controversy which soon outgrows the immediate issue and encompasses larger differences. Similarly, the use of suspenders initiates disagreement among members, but these are soon forgotten in entangling arguments. In this way, however, jewelry, gadgets, or styles attain religious significance, perhaps stand as symbols of "Meidung" or separation, much as relics, altars, and vestments caused violent upheavals during the early Reformation. Each item of dispute or debate may engender such Christian indignation that the people involved may sever all communication and relationship. It is also possible to find a father who rides to church with his wife in his horse-drawn carriage, while the son drives his family in an automobile to a much larger congregation; or that a son uses tractor and electric lights, while the parents in a wing of the same home use kerosene lamps. In such a family, peace prevails. Although the father bemoans the son's worldliness, the son respects his parents' ways of living.

The large unaffiliated Oak Grove Mennonite Church in

Green Township, Wayne County, could itself easily be the subject of a study in the adaptation and acculturation of a religious group. The congregation was Old Order Amish when its members settled in the thick forest land in 1812. Since that time it has had a phenomenal growth in both size and influence; it has, however, been plagued by schisms and division over the years. The original core of the church membership has remained true to the central tenets of Mennonite doctrine but has also adapted itself slowly to changes in the American scene.

In the past the congregation has debated such questions as whether to accept or reject a common meetinghouse, a Sunday school, Sunday evening services, evangelistic or revival meetings, baptism in church or in running water, rebaptism upon reception of other Mennonite groups, marriage between Mennonites of differing districts, or a seminary-trained clergy. Such unrelated items as the custom of being photographed, barber haircuts, modern clothes, brewing of beer, resistance to civilian authority, use of the "Ausbund" or a modern hymnal, four-part singing, musical instruments, and the use of German or English in the Sunday service or school, have all caused dissension. The majority of the Oak Grove congregation has always favored a gradual and moderate acceptance of prevailing trends. Many of the groups which separated from Oak Grove cannot now be identified by their *raison d'être*, but the Oak Grove Church is as strong and influential as ever.

The Oak Grove congregation is, moreover, one of the wealthiest and most intellectually eminent Mennonite congregations in America. Its growth to independence may be traced to the development of the inner capabilities and resources of its members. The General Conference Mennonite body has regarded this church as too progressive to be included in its membership, but, in spite of this action, Oak Grove members still give energetic and practical support to causes sponsored by the Mennonite group at large. Without remuneration, for example, Howard Yoder of

Wooster, owner of a thriving greenhouse in Wayne County, has twice taken a year's leave from his business to serve in relief projects in Europe after World War I and II. Enterprising church members have supported Mennonite refugee relief, heifer projects, community meat canning for overseas distribution, civilian public service camps, and CROP activities.

The minister of Oak Grove until 1959, Vergil M. Gerig, a personable young man, is a College of Wooster graduate with a degree in divinity from Princeton Theological Seminary. Other church members have been graduated from the College of Wooster and from leading Mennonite colleges, such as Goshen in Indiana and Bluffton in Ohio, and have become university professors, doctors, and high-level government officials. Jacob C. Meyer, professor-emeritus of history, Western Reserve University, Roy C. Wenger, professor of visual education, Kent State University, Dr. O. C. Yoder, and Dr. James Steiner represent this group.[12]

In government service on an international level is O. Ben Gerig, former assistant executive secretary of the League of Nations, now American representative to the Trusteeship Council of the United Nations. Younger members of the church are also rising to places of eminence in the field of education and in the other professions. The Oak Grove Church is unique in its particular development and history; in externals it has often gone with the times. Its heart remains firm to the Mennonite faith. Its record of accomplishment and Christian concern for needy and displaced persons of the world rivals that of any existing Protestant denomination today.

In contrast with Oak Grove are the many Old Order Amish districts which have not changed. These have chosen to brace themselves as consistently as possible against modern cultural advance with an outright negative response. Their answer to freedom and opportunity has always been a vigorous "No." They have acquired land and moved to regions where land was available, but change has stopped with that. They have saved themselves much annoyance and have preserved their unique identity by adopting a totally negative, defensive attitude from the first encounter. This seems to have given them the strength, if not the right, to resist all further encroachments with greater ease and less upheaval. In fact one has come to expect the negative response from the Amish. They would not be Amish if they did react positively. Federal and state regulations on crops, barn improvements, taxes and social security, and school attendance certainly have influenced them. But to the introduction of such items as electricity, telephone, automobile, radio, tractor, safety razor, the standardization of manufactured wearing apparel, the reply is a vigorous "No."

Merely from outward appearance and mode of transportation several types of Mennonites may be distinguished on the streets of Wooster. Men with untrimmed beards riding in frail surreys are unmistakably Old Order Amish. If the horse-drawn carriage, however, carries a clean-shaven man, he is a Wissler Mennonite from the northwestern section of the county. Men with fairly long beards, but trimmed along the edges, who drive automobiles are "Conservative Amish" or Church Amish. If the beards are mere semblances of growth around lower cheek and chin and the mode of transportation is the automobile, the church affiliation is undoubtedly Old Order Mennonite. Of the remaining Mennonites only the kind of coat may be a distinguishing mark. Some conferences still insist on a coat without lapel and a shirt without a necktie. These distinguishing marks are now fast disappearing, leaving the Old Order Amish, unworldly, resistant to change, unique in the modern culture, and an exciting subject of observation and research.

THE OLD ORDER AMISH

The Old Order Amish, the most conservative element in the large Mennonite denomination, make excellent copy for Sunday supplement writers and editors; the latter, naturally, highlight "newsworthy" items, but the Amish deserve more penetrating attention. Again, when state and federal agencies clash occasionally with the Amish over matters of social security, acreage limitation, or compulsory school attendance, local and national publicity immediately focuses on Amish faces and buggies. These people do not seek publicity, and they do not want to disagree with the law. However, as a community which makes every attempt to stand still while the surrounding society moves forward, the Amish inevitably find conflict, if not with people, then with the ever-increasing mesh of external regulation by governmental bureaus and agencies. The attempt to understand the source of their unique position in the modern age is both necessary and rewarding. At the same time it shows that the Amish do not stand as still as they frequently seem to do.

The Old Order Amish distinguish themselves from the rest of the Mennonites by their definition of the "world," not by a difference in confessional doctrines. They cling tenaciously to a literal interpretation of the New Testament injunction of the separation of God's elect from the world (II Cor. 6:14–18). The sixteenth-century Swiss Brethren, Anabaptist predecessors of both Amish and Mennonites, drafted their Confession of Faith on February 24, 1527, in Schleitheim near Schaffhausen on the Rhine. Fourth, and most significant for our study, among its seven cardinal points is:

> A separation shall be made from the evil and from the wickedness which the devil planted in the world; in this manner, simply, that we shall not have fellowship with them and not run with them in the multitude of their abominations. . . .
>
> To us, then, the command of the Lord is clear when He calls upon us to separate from the evil, and thus He will be our God and we shall be His sons and daughters.

He further admonishes us to withdraw from Babylon and the earthly Egypt that we may not be partakers of the pain and suffering which the Lord will bring upon them. . . .[13]

Separation, as laid down in this earliest confession, is still valid today. The Mennonite General Conference of 1921 expressed its agreement with it in Article X of its *Christian Fundamentals*:

Of Separation

We believe that we are called with a holy calling to a life of separation from the world and its follies, sinful practices, and methods; further that it is the duty of the Church to keep herself aloof from all movements which seek the reformation of society independent of the merits of the death of Christ and the experience of the new birth. I Pet. 2:9; Tit. 2:11–14; II Cor. 6:14–18; Rom. 12:1, 2; Eph. 5:11; I John 2:15–17; II Thess. 2:6; Acts 4:12; John 3:3, 6, 7.[14]

The variance between the Old Order Amish and most Mennonite conferences lies in the interpretation and degree of application of the rule of separation. The Amish, untutored and unschooled in their leadership as in their membership, interpret literally whatever doctrine and biblical passage they have once come to accept. The entire gamut of Amish idiosyncracies as perceived at the present day stands and falls with these articles of separation.

After his death in 1907, David A. Treyer, bishop for fifty-six years in an Old Order Amish district in Ohio, left a few writings as a rare testimony of Amish thought and preaching. In his *Hinterlassene Schriften* he writes (my translation):

For although there are nowadays peculiarly many constitutions [i.e., Mennonite], and almost each one praises his own as the best, nevertheless we can conclude from the everlasting word of God, if we honestly and impartially examine it, that many are built only on sand, yes, almost all of them, except those of the so-called Old Amish and the Old Mennonite. These are still a relic of the old apostolic community, which, as we can find in faithful descriptions, was almost completely destroyed and disintegrated at certain times. But under the wise guidance and power of God, through devout men like Menno Simons and Dietrich Phillip and others, the community of God has been reformed again and has been built and founded on the immovable ground and cornerstone Jesus Christ, and now regrettably again for reasons given above in part so far deviated.[15]

The separation from the world demands of the Amish the avoidance of social, political, and religious intercourse with modern America. Economic communication is allowed: these people do business with "Yankees" in their daily farm life. But the separation extends to differences in dress and personal appearance and the refusal to accept many home and farm appliances in common usage. An Amish man, therefore, does not attend gatherings within the city, modern places of amusement, motion picture houses, dance halls, taverns, or even the county fair. He may take his family to see a city, to visit a zoo, to a railroad or bus station, to the city dime store, hardware, or drugstore. While he is in the city he may shop for his groceries and refresh himself and his children with ice cream cones. But he visits no relatives in the city and certainly does not attend city churches. Nor does he vote, as a rule, in either county, state, or national elections. He may, however, be persuaded to participate in voting on school and county bond issues which concern his locality. He swears no oaths and takes up no arms in defense of himself or his country.

He is accustomed to keeping his house unlocked. He does not pursue the criminal attacker; he does keep his fences

straight and his house and yard in order. He does not adorn his home with mirrors, photographs, pictures, wallpaper, lace curtains, or "fancy" upholstered furniture; he paints his rooms in one color and covers his floor with linoleum or leaves it bare. His kitchen is not a miracle of modern devices, but it is a model of cleanliness and order. He works his farm with horse-drawn equipment and human power.

More subtle are the implications of separation when it comes to avoidance of organizations of every kind, including those which are associated with modern church life. The Amish today, as in the past, do not support

> a single rural, home or foreign mission station or relief project—not a Sunday school, not an evening meeting, not a Bible conference, a summer Bible school, a Young People's Meeting, an academy, college or Bible school, a church-publishing house or a church periodical, an orphan's home, a home for the aged, a hospital, a district mission board, a relief organization—nothing, except the local congregational organization, the church service with periodic observance of the ordinances, informal Sunday visiting, informal Sunday evening social gatherings for young people, and more or less informal visits of preachers and bishops to pioneer settlements scattered along the frontier.[16]

Their own severest critic, Joseph W. Yoder, a former member of a Pennsylvania Amish community, stated that "Das alt Gebrauch (the old custom) definitely prevents all progress in the religious life, no Sunday school, no Bible class instruction, but everything as it always was." Then he added these significant words: "Jakob Amman seems to have taught his followers, What we have adopted now [ca. 1693] is absolutely right and any departure from this Ordnung is and forever will be wrong."[17] And so it is.

The failure to support missions causes considerable debate unfavorable to the Amish. Their own peculiar way of

34

reasoning on this matter may be illustrated by the sermons of the aforementioned Bishop Treyer:

> I understand the Old Mennonites and many other groups are unanimous in this affair [i.e., missions] and believe the command to the apostles to go out into all the world to preach the gospel to all peoples etc. belongs to all teachers and preachers. Answer: If this is our calling, then woe to us and to many who were before us. But with much reading and thinking I find until now as yet not a sufficient reason in the word of God to affirm this assertion.
>
> For we are no apostles, but only shepherds and teachers. And therefore our profession is also not the same. The word apostle means an emissary, and I do not find that the apostles have again affirmed other apostles, or have sent out somebody else with the command which they themselves had from the Lord. But they occupied the congregations with preachers and elders, with the command, that they should pasture the herd above which they were set. (Acts 20:28; I Peter 5:2.) And Paul says: God has set up in the congregation first the apostles, then the prophets, and thirdly teachers. (I Corinthians 12:28.) And again: And he had ordained some as apostles, some however as prophets, some as evangelists, some as shepherds and teachers. (Ephesians 4:11.) Therefore, we are far removed from the time of the apostles and their office. And so likewise from the miracles and strange signs and forces, with which they were endowed and gifted, in order to fulfill their vocation and to do what was commanded of them.[18]

Amish taboos also include secret societies, civic organizations, political clubs, life and fire insurance companies, and membership and affiliation with U.S. government-sponsored agricultural agencies. On a voluntary basis the Amish have restricted certain crop acreage, but they have refused to accept government compensation for not planting. Those

35

of their group who have worked in the employ of contractors have paid their social security deductions, but some cases are known where benefits have been refused. Two Amish men are known to have belonged to the Wooster and Fredericksburg Alcoholics Anonymous. One of them, a Mose Yoder, became a favorite speaker with other Ohio groups. Because he had to travel considerably on behalf of A.A., he has now severed his affiliation with the Old Order Amish group and has moved into a locality of Ohio where the ownership of cars is permitted. But the Fredericksburg group still has Amish members.

Since 1955, all farmers, including Old Order Amish, have been required to pay social security taxes to the United States government. Many Amish consistently failed to do so, because they were against all forms of insurance, and this tax seemed to them a form of life insurance. Life insurance to the Amish means taking a gamble on human life, which to them is a gift of God who in turn allows no gamble with his gifts. Special meetings between federal revenue agents and Amish leaders brought about some quiet acceptance of the law, but a considerable number of individual Amishmen would not comply under any condition. During September, 1958, the U.S. Department of Internal Revenue filed liens on horses, cattle, and bank accounts of Amish who were not paying their social security tax. Again more Amishmen, but not all of them, complied with the law. Finally, on October 8, 1958, government agents took into custody twenty-nine horses and one cow to be auctioned in order to bring in the delinquent payments. In two public sales, advertised according to custom and held in neighboring Canton, the Internal Revenue Department satisfied its claims, but the Amish were not the buyers of the horses or the cow. The Amish have gained wide national sympathy in their desire to remain free of social security taxes and benefits. At this writing a case is pending in the United States Supreme Court, and Senator Frank Lausche

(Democrat, Ohio) is actively championing their plea in Congress.

A listing of the members of the Old Order Amish community in Wayne, Holmes, Tuscarawas, and Coshocton counties as recorded by Deacon Ervin Gingerich of Millersburg, Ohio, in the *Ohio Amish Directory*, Volume I, 1959, gives a total membership of 3,812. To this figure may be added the 569 members of splinter groups, making a total of 4,371 Old Order Amish in these four Ohio counties. Three family names, Miller, Yoder, and Troyer, have more baptized members (909) than all the other forty families together (720). Paradoxically there are eight families whose name appears only once—Anderson, Byler, Frey, Glick, Helmuth, Hilty, Petersheim, and Zook. At the same time it may be noted that only three Amish names—Bontrager, Helmuth, and Nisley—are not found in the Wooster city telephone directory for 1960. The above list is evidence that certain Amish family names are mainly found only in a few areas within the United States, that the Amish have tended to migrate by families, and that marriage into the group does occur.

It is interesting to compare with these figures the registrations of Local Draft Board No. 1, Millersburg, Holmes County, Ohio. There were listed in 1945 412 Millers, 167 Yoders, 104 Troyers, 68 Masts, 64 Rabers, 62 Schlabachs, 52 Weavers, 39 Beachys, etc.

According again to statistics compiled by Deacon Gingerich, the Old Order Amish showed a decrease in baptized membership during 1960. The disturbingly large number of defections from the Old Order were caused by the growing insistence upon the right to own an automobile or tractor. A new "Bethel Fellowship" was formed in the very heart of the Amishland by members of Old Order districts who aim, in the home and in outward appearance, to preserve the inheritance of the fathers but wish to adapt themselves in other ways to a faster tempo in the competitive world.

Rarely does an Amishman as a single individual venture forth alone into a locality not previously settled by Amish people. Several go together to found a colony. In one instance, an individual family which had gone to a different section of the region returned within a very short time to the safe inclosure of the group. Again, three young families of one Amish district, who had dispersed into the outside "world" a few years before, safely retreated to the rural environment of their Amish district; they were welcomed and accepted as lost sheep come home. Concomitantly, the threats of severance and isolation, the force of the "Meidung," the ban, the "mite," shunning, of being set apart or ousted from all intercourse, extending to the very table, hearth, and bed, and with it the privation of help on the farm—all this as an outgrowth of breach of mores—are effective means of keeping the district united and the individual safe from apostasy.

The cohesiveness so characteristic of the Amish has led to what the "Yankee" neighbors may call "clannishness," and actual cases of the "freezing-out" of non-Amish farmers are on record. These incidents of apparent hostility must be considered as economic rather than social in nature. As an example, if only one non-Amish farmer lives along a country road, it is obvious that neither he nor the power company can afford to provide telephone or electric lines; therefore the non-Amish must move to another locality unless he wishes to share the Amish lack of power facilities.

The self-sufficiency and solidarity of the Old Order Amish districts, on the other hand, are so extensive that no member of a congregation has ever come under the care of any county or national relief agency. Criminal charges against any member of the sect are likewise unknown. Only the "mite" case of 1945 (see chap. iv, " 'Meidung' in Modern Times") and several school cases are recorded in the local courthouse. Any member showing tendencies toward unaccustomed or irregular behavior is disciplined within the community. The rulers of the district keep a watchful eye over their flock. Non-conformists are warned in private, then brought to the attention of the "Gemei"; if they still persist in their individualistic behavior, they are expelled from the congregation. On the other hand, the overseers give counsel and help to the needy. A widow with children is urged to remarry, and eligible men are suggested. Orphaned children are never sent to institutions and therefore are no burden on the local welfare authority. Living on alms or on the fruits of somebody else's labor is not tolerated. Everybody, male and female, capable of giving physical assistance is required to do so. The old people never sell out to retire to the city; instead they stay where they have always been—and if they cannot work any longer, their presence brings inspiration and comfort to younger members of the family. At the same time, each family provides for its sick and aged. If illness should cause an unmanageable hardship, then the district comes forward with aid.

Separation from the world for the Old Order Amish requires, therefore, a retreat to a life in a rural environment within a limited and narrowly circumscribed locality. It implies the preservation of manners and customs which the group has come to recognize as characteristic of separation from the world. When the author asked an Amish official whether he could become an Amishman, the answer was quick and decisive: "Yes, if you take off these clothes and become a farmer." Transgressions of its boundaries are permissible only for business reasons and for a limited time, and a return to the inner fold is always taken for granted. A concomitant phenomenon of this strict separation and isolation, as witnessed in several instances in Ohio, are the Swartzentruber, Stutzman, and King districts of Old Order Amish, which refuse and abstain from any association even with other Amish districts. In these groups the peasant mentality with its attendant conservatism seems to have ossified to an even more extreme degree of self-sufficiency and self-righteousness. Assimilation to the surrounding world engenders considerable conflict among these groups.

Several men and one woman belonging to these groups were sent to the county jail during the winter of 1960 because, under threat of proscription by their bishop, they had failed to comply with the traffic laws of Ohio which required more than a kerosene light on their buggies.

When the Amish clash with the public law, it is the Amish who must revise their ways. Their mores may claim religious sanction, but, as in the cases of stronger buggy lights just mentioned, Amish religious sanction must give way. Governmental directives of state and national compass encroach upon the most remote farmstead, and neither the strongest religious nor rural mores can be impervious to such embracing controls. On the other hand, many of the inroads and invasions which the outer world makes upon the Amish come not by conscious acceptance but by the slow process of unconscious absorption and infiltration. The Amish may not want to be of this world; nevertheless they cannot retreat entirely and hermetically. All men share to a greater or lesser degree in the culture patterns of a national society.

The Amish believe that restrictions and hardships in this earthly life are necessary. Furthermore they are firmly convinced that, the more restrictions and burdens they set upon themselves, the more assured they may be of eternal salvation. These thoughts are the marrow of their preaching. Bishop Treyer gave them full expression when he stated that Christian churches had to be "fenced in" (umzäunt) by rules (Ordnung), for without this spiritual "fence" (Zaun) no community can long exist.[19] The objection one may hear now and then is that the Amish life is all "fence," but the Amish are convinced that, the higher and thicker the "fence" and the harder their toil here on earth, the better they are as Amishmen.

The "fence" or Zaun concept of the Amish bears a double significance or acts like a double-edged sword. The fence not only guards against intrusion from without, but, more than that, it protects, unifies, and lends strength to those within its circumference. This second aspect bears the greater weight. The isolation and abstention from modern organizational life seems possible only on the basis of a consciousness of this kind. Without the assurance of equality embodied in this district solidarity, without mutual sympathy and aid in case of need, the Amish man and woman could not survive. Their strength lies in the unity of the group, in the uniformity of its customs, in the likeness of appearance, in the sameness of setting and activity, in the proximity of their farmsteads, in the goals and purposes, thoughts, beliefs, and practices enjoined upon all members of the one "Gemei," or district. Through this oneness of life, they survive. The next chapter tells how the Old Order Amish live within this unity.

CHAPTER II

THE AMISH HOMESTEAD

House and Barn

Central Ohio's countryside is at once appealing: its well-kept, large farmyards, fertile fields, pastures, and wooded areas please the eye. Nature's own rich endowment, coupled with the farmer's industry, has created in this region a civilization recognizable as the best America has to offer. The pioneer who came brought the image of a prosperous future with him: he cleared the woods and plowed his newly won fields; he raised his lines of demarcation and set his goals; he built a home and shelter for all he owned; and he did not abandon these after a brief success. Soil and climate sided with his strength and endurance; to this day crop failures and sheriff's sales are unknown. The farmer of this region is as much an entrepreneur as is his neighbor in the surrounding industrial cities.

Settlers in the forest wilderness placed their homesteads near the center of their future activities. Material for home building stood all around; it was the pioneer's for the taking. Many of the first cabins of the region remain to this

day. Many are still inhabited, some now dressed up with white clapboard to resemble newer farm homes. But bulging sides and the slant of window frames often reveal an original log construction. Typically, when the family outgrew the log hut, the owner erected a larger house, made of brick burned in the farmyard. Sandstone houses in Wayne County are so rare they can be counted on the fingers of one hand.

The farmer of German descent preferred a narrow rectangular frame house. To this day it is the predominant type in central Ohio. A lower story, half concealed on an incline, serves as both kitchen and cellar. The food supply is thus always close at hand and in a good state of natural refrigeration. The central entrance door to both basement and first story anchors the symmetrical arrangement of windows on each side. If an Amishman now buys a house with large one-piece window panes, he soon removes them and substitutes small sections. A porch runs across the entire length of the three-room first story. To the rear of the house a similar porch is inclosed to form the bedroom of the parents and a pantry or storage room. An added upper floor provides bed space for the usually numerous members of the family. The gables of the house are low but contain one or two small windows or even a glass-covered six-paneled star. Chimneys are few in number, for no peace is promised to a home with more chimneys on the roof than women in the house. A good coat of white paint on all buildings and on the fences surrounding the yard is a characteristic of the "Dutch" country. Occasionally barn and outbuildings gleam in bright red, but that color is rare as one approaches the Amish country. Elaborately decorated farm buildings are not seen; to paint the house or barn or the window frames and shutters in different colors is now most unusual.

To recognize an Amish home, one need only look for the presence of the horse and buggy, or, if this should fail, a glance at the windows may tell the faith of the inhabitants. Plain blue or green cloth curtains are the unmistakable characteristic of the Amish. Lace or ruffled curtains are taboo.

The "grossvater" or "granddaddy house" is another characteristic of Amishland. Smaller than the family home, it is often its duplicate; at times it is a wing added, or an extension built, to the side of the house. The proximity of the two houses is very striking; often they are connected by a catwalk. Amish grandparents do not retire to the city; they vacate their home instead to a younger child. On the scene of their own greatest activity, the grandparents watch the family of one of their children grow, sharing still, in their own way, in the bustle of an active farm life. Both houses are remarkable, of course, for their immaculate whiteness, set off by a surrounding of healthy turf and abundant flowers. A vigorously cultivated kitchen garden supplies both homes.

The interior of the typical Amish home is very clean, though somewhat chilling because of the meagerness of the furnishings. The curtains of solid-colored blue or green cloth, the oilcloth on the eating table, the few, unmatched chairs, the odd cutlery, the plain chinaware, or even tin or enameled plates, the iron bedstead in the almost bare bedroom—all suggest the chaste frugality and restrained modesty of the Amish. Overstuffed, colored, modern furniture is absent. A corner cupboard, or an old commode perhaps, contain all the household possessions of the family. These scant but necessary items the Amish buy at the numerous weekly auctions held regularly throughout the region. On an Amish moving day, a single farm wagon can easily transport the entire belongings of a family.

The absence of all pictures or portraits of present or past generations, of all other wall decorations, including wallpaper, of rugs or carpets, of knickknacks or art objects, of fancy quilts, covers, or pillowcases heightens the impression of sobriety and austerity. Television sets, radios, hi-fi combinations, phonographs, and musical instruments are taboo.

45

No electric gadgets clutter up their kitchens. An odd table may hold a few religious books, including the big family Bible in German and perhaps the local newspaper. Magazines are noticeably absent, though the Mennonite bimonthly *Harold der Wahrheit* reaches a few homes. The Sugarcreek *Budget* brings weekly news from every other Amish district and from faraway settlements. In this plainness is a sense of order and pride. Floors, ceilings, and walls, customarily painted in gray oil paint, are immaculate. The cast-iron stove shines with polishing. On the kitchen windowsill are boxes of blooming plants.

Tradition demands that when an Amishman buys a modern farm he remove all electric wiring, central heating, and perhaps even running water. The kitchen tap, however, is generally favored over the old-fashioned hand pump and the heavy stone sink. If house and farm are mortgaged, however, the former owner as a rule prevents the removal of utility installations until the debt is liquidated. Some Amish, it is said, have thus come to appreciate electricity; it is ʿlaimed that they have deferred final payment in some instances until the bishop interfered.

As an example of approved Amish inventiveness, there is the case of the family which bought an abandoned schoolyard and built their home near its artesian spring. The flow of the water was found to be strong enough to power a water wheel in the basement of the house. This in turn pumped water into an attic tank which supplied both kitchen and barn troughs. Bathtubs are slowly making their way into Amish homes. Lately the Amish have also begun to use bottled gas. This convenience has induced some of them to invest in cooking stoves and refrigerators. So far no general proscription of this type of gas appliance has been issued. At the same time, although many natural gas and electric power lines run through the territory, church regulations forbid the tapping of these sources. But the gasoline lamp, which gives a brighter light than the kerosene, is much used.

The large two-storied bank or Swiss barn is the marvel of the German settlement. The German farmer introduced and developed this type of farm building on the American scene. Under one roof he concentrates all his indoor work and shelters all his animals, his grain, his feed, and his implements. This economy of operation he has learned from long experience. After all, his farm is his wealth, the means of his livelihood, the very reason of his existence, and the barn is the symbol and content of that enterprise. In the European homeland of the Alps, the Black Forest, or the Jura regions, inclement weather and the scarcity of land and materials had forced him to economy and concentration of labor and housing. There, even today, the dwelling place is part of the one-roof farm structure. But to put home and barn under one roof, with the home occupying a tier of rooms at one end of the building, proved unnecessary on the American frontier. Moreover, the exigencies of settling in the forest wilderness compelled the settler to separate his home from the shelter for his livestock and feed, at least at first.

The first demand upon the pioneer was to erect a shelter and home for his family. His isolation in the woods made him build the home with materials at hand. Stone of any kind was absent, but, by using the choicest timber selected from oak, hickory, ash, and walnut, he could build to outlast his own life span. Then too, the availability of cheap land and wood encouraged him to think of aggrandizing his holdings and of dispersing his work buildings. He could gauge the size of his barn by the extent of his ultimate goals. The future magnitude and the fertility of his fields, the number of horses he would need, the herd of cows to be milked and properly cared for, all these determined the dimensions of the barn. In addition, before the advent of the combine, large storage spaces and wide threshing dens were indispensable for the quality wheat for which the region was especially renowned. To this day one may delight in the solid black walnut planks, two inches thick and

thirty inches high, or in the cherry wood boards wider than any tree now seems capable of growth which line the sides of these dens.

Besides the extensive mows for the wheat harvest, the "Dutch" farmer needed room in his barn for the hay and straw for his animals' bedding. Through conveniently placed openings in the floor, he supplied the stable below. The German farmer has always treated his animals as prudently and cautiously as he treats himself. Good bedding preserves a healthy stock. Besides it makes for good manure which has always been essential to his way of farming. The experience of the generations has taught him that the quality of a harvest corresponds to the amount of fertilizer used. Therefore the farmer keeps his straw where it can most easily be supplied—in the spacious barn.

Another virtue of the bank barn is that its large superstructure prevents too rapid fluctuations of temperature in the stable below. Sudden variability in heat and cold is recognized as detrimental to livestock. Furthermore, as opposed to the "flat" or "Yankee" one-story barn, these large, almost grandiose structures—often with a width of 50 feet and length of 114 feet—are so wide that a team pulling a harvest wagon up the ramp or bank is able to turn around inside. Some barns have as many as four threshing dens plus the mows at either end. Nowadays, new methods of harvesting and the tendency to concentrate upon one crop make many of these barns obsolete. Only in the Amishland do they survive at all, incontestable, almost ostentatious landmarks of the German influence. To this day they remain visible testimony to the ambition and wealth of the owners.

The builders of bank barns experimented throughout the first century on the Ohio frontier to find the most lasting and serviceable type of barn construction. Was the roof, for instance, to be low and fairly flat, as is that of the Alpine house which retains heavy layers of snow as protective covering? Was it to be steep, like that of the straw-thatched roof of

48

the Black Forest house, to facilitate the quick flow of rain or melting snow? The changeable climate of Ohio, thawing deep snows quickly in sudden bright sunlight, found the one-quarter or one-third pitch (pitch is the relation of height of the gable to the width of the barn) inappropriate. The shingle-covered roofs deteriorated too quickly. There-fore, one-half and even full pitch—gable height equal to barn width—proved more lasting. Only later did the aca-demically trained builder corroborate this design by show-ing how much faster the volume of storage space increases with a full-pitch roof. But the human arm is too weak to lift straw and hay to such heights. The hip-and saddle roof thus came into favor.

The location and placing of the barn in relation to the house and the rest of the farm was also considered. House and barn usually stand at right angles to each other, with a southern exposure preferable for the house. To create natu-ral drainage, the barn usually stands on an incline in the contour of the landscape. The axis of the barn runs gener-ally from south to north, thereby exposing its smallest ex-panse, the barn doors above the bank or ramp, to the pre-dominantly western winds. The frame of the inner struc-ture thus stands braced east and west. Though lightning and fires take their yearly toll, no bank barn is ever known to have been blown down. Roofs have been ripped off, but the heavy hand-hewn white oak timbers are joiced and pecked so precisely that no force of wind has been able to shake them loose. Similarly their faultless stem timber has so far withstood all assaults except those of fire. Beams of one piece support the whole width of the floor, and often they extend six feet over the unsupported east side of the stables. In this way the second floor, with its characteristic overshoot, affords a shelter against rain and sunshine for the animals in the barnyard.

The barn siding, too, formed the subject of much experi-mentation. The oldest barns had green oak boards running vertically the full height of the barn. Upon drying, this green

49

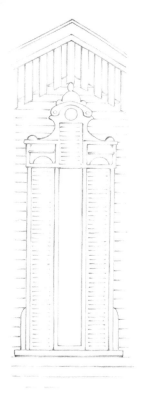

wood shrank, leaving interstices advantageous for the curing of the hay but detrimental to the wheat harvest. At times, therefore, one finds them covered with narrow strips. Later in the nineteenth century the siding was set horizontally to conform with that of the farm house. It was found, however, that when the barn stood unprotected against the rain the moisture would settle under the boards and rot them. Some prosperous farmers then covered their barns with siding of white pine, which of course is not native to the region.

The ventilation of the barn, necessary for the curing of hay and for the harvest, became a matter of much concern. The oldest barns have no openings or windows. Later square, shuttered openings were installed at measured intervals. Two rows were found to increase the effectiveness of the arrangement. Gradually these openings were so lengthened as to merge into one long window almost the full height of the middle section. Both shutters and glass were used in them; the shutters for ventilation, the glass for lighting. Without exception these windows were adorned with fancy scrollwork and pointed arches. In them the builder created the semblance of a Gothic cathedral, and many of these barns have indeed been mistaken for churches. In summertime, of course, they do serve as churches for the Amish.

The farmer, as a rule, placed tiny openings in the gable in the form of a sun, half moon, five-pointed star, cross, or three crosses or diamonds. There is nothing fancy or elaborate in these symbols, commonly known as "hex signs." Nothing of the intricate, large, and gaily colored Pennsylvania barn decorations is found in Ohio. In fact, the openings in the gable are often so small that only the trained observer will detect them.

These symbols belong to that same strand of folk religion whereby the old Germanic, pre-Christian householder affixed the symbols of two horses' heads atop his house or stable in honor of Wotan, god of all farm life. Thereby he

50

placed his homestead under the protection of Wotan's power. The Roman Catholic farmer to this very day may use palm branches, blessed by the priest, to guard his possessions from the harm of evil influences and the Protestant builder may affix Christian or nature insignia on his home or barn. The ever-present three windows or tripartite large window in the triangle of the gable of the bank barn—assuring the veneration and protection of the Trinity—is another manifestation of folk religion. As a rule, when this type of window is absent, the smaller "hex signs" are found. The Amishman will not tell whether he knows the significance of these signs. In one instance an Amish preacher cut a large star into his own new barn. His claim that the opening served merely to ventilate the barn was rather dubious, since a simple square opening would have served this purpose far better than an intricate pentagram. The remark of another owner that the iron cross-like cutout was "for the birds" certainly was an evasive answer. The Amish do not allow lightning rods on any of their buildings. Most necessary, therefore, are the Christian symbols to withstand attacks by evil powers like lightning, wind, or disease. The disbelief or ignorance of the significance of these traditional protective symbols on the part of the occasional non-Amish occupant of these houses and farms points out how the European peasant has gradually developed on the American scene into the modern farmer. The latter, in his undertakings, no longer pays heed to phases of sun and moon and the signs of the zodiac; he does not fear the demonic influence of evil spirits or implore the benevolence of the Christian religion and the Trinity. The modern agriculturist as capitalistic, scientifically trained entrepreneur relies more on credit from the local bank, the latest recommendations of the Experiment Station, governmental bulletins, experiments by scientists, the long-range weather forecasts, and market reports, as well as on his own power-equipped operations. The Amish are chary in using them.

It has been indicated before that the Amish are able to lead their kind of life with less interference and temptation the further they are removed into the hills of Wayne and adjacent Holmes counties. Even the size of families seems to increase the greater the distance between the Amish and modernity. To speak of "large" families is rather an understatement. Ralph Ely, as principal of Applecreek High School in East Union Township, Wayne County, in sampling twenty-five families represented in his school, found the number of Amish children to be 9.67 per family. This was in 1932 before the national birth rate had begun to rise, but even today the figure seems to hold true for the Amish. They abhor interference with the God-given, natural way of procreation. One Amishman expressed his group's philosophy of life when he stated that it was good for a woman to bear a child each year as it was for a cow to freshen yearly. (Parenthetically it must be mentioned that the Ohio Amish do not employ mules because they are hybrids and usually sterile.)

A young Amish couple begins its venture in farming on a small scale. If their union is blessed with increase, survival as a family unit dictates expansion. The epitome of growth climaxes in a maximum of about a quarter section of land, or approximately 160 acres.

Children are a gift of God. Children are also an economic asset and a necessity on a farm dependent for its operation on human and animal power. Upon the birth of a child the American peasant seems in no way different from his European counterpart who will ask: "What is it good for?" The Amish have not changed in this respect through the centuries. Benjamin Rush remarked about the German settlers of Pennsylvania before the turn of the century:

> The favorite influence on agriculture, as conducted by the Germans . . . is manifested by the joy they ex-

press upon the birth of a child. No dread of poverty nor distrust of Providence, from an increasing family, depresses the spirits of these industrious and frugal people. Upon the birth of a son, they exult in the gift of a ploughman or a wagoner; upon the birth of a daughter they rejoice in the addition of another spinster or milk maid to the family.[1]

Though they rejoice at the birth, the Amish have little time later to play with their children. As an Amish mother of twelve living children expressed it: "We have little time to love our children."

The Amish entrepreneur remains a small operator unless he increases his own cheapest supply of human labor. Small families, and there are a few, live on small farm holdings. One man with one team of horses is restricted by the amount of work he can do. When the Amishman asserts that he must be bigger than his land, he means to say: a small plot of land well cultivated produces more than extensive acres which cannot be worked for lack of proper help. To expand his operations with reliance on hired help is too costly. But a father who has growing sons will search for a larger farm and acquire additional teams of horses and milk cows to keep these hands busy. Amish and non-Amish farms equal each other in ambition and pride in productiveness and size of undertaking, but the Amish farmer is handicapped because he cannot rely on motorization; yet, since his life on the farm is his only way to heaven, he cannot abandon it for a pursuit in the city.

The severest threat to the growth and expansion of the Amish community arises with the scarcity of land. The inherent productivity of the farms throughout the region and their proximity to urban centers have made them objects of investment or speculation. In spite of pooling their financial resources at times, the Amish cannot adequately compete in the bidding. Thus, while in general farm land tends to concentrate in ever larger holdings, fewer farms appear

53

on the market now, and Amish farms, on the contrary, are being carved up more and more in order to offer sons and daughters opportunities to establish themselves as new economic and family units. Another consequence of the scarcity of land is to make the Amish move to other parts of the state and country. Then, too, Amish fathers and older children often are forced to seek employment away from home as carpenters, painters, brick masons, or laborers in quarries, sawmills, or strip mines. The wife and younger children have to finish the everyday chores. And, even in Amishland, general farming is giving way to intensive or specialized efforts such as potato farming, dairying, or poultry raising. The Amish share in the pride of Wayne County as the chief dairy, chicken, and potato county of Ohio.

Amish children are work forces before they have physically matured and before they have finished their formal schooling. As part and parcel of the farm they are intrusted with appropriate tasks. According to Amish thinking, a boy does not have to be sixteen years of age or to have finished school before he can guide a harrow; long before that time necessity requires him to shuck wheat or corn, or to distribute feed and bedding to the livestock. The Amish arguments for a school year shorter than nine months and against compulsory attendance to the age of sixteen (the Amish youngster leaves school on the very day he reaches that age) of course conflict with formal and institutionalized education. Innately these people believe that a peasant belongs behind the plow, not behind a schoolbook, and that the barn is not built to sit in.

Education in the public high school leads to a new life, one often hostile to country living. Therefore the Amish induce their children to work from earliest youth, and they try to prevent their being weaned away from home. As integral parts of the farm Amish boys and girls must grow in harmony with the enterprise. To be sure the modern school with its diverse curriculum offers distractions to them. Much of modern education, in the Amish view, is useless and inessential to a farming project. Besides, they say, the children do not need to know more than father and grandfather know; have they not prospered in life? "The peasant believes only his father"; thus runs a well-known proverb. Hence, apart from reading, writing, and arithmetic, which an Amishman also needs to know, the dictum: "je gelehrter, desto verkehrter"—"the more learned, the more confused"—is a bit of peasant wisdom which he interprets in his own righteous manner. The Amish see no reproach in the city dweller's reply: "Die dümmsten Bauern haben die dicksten Kartoffeln"—"The dumbest peasants have the biggest potatoes."

Many Amish boys and girls, of course, milk several cows and do other chores before they take their long way on foot or by buggy to school. Similar tasks await them on their return. The Amish cannot agree to transport their children in a motorized school bus and then have them take physical exercise as part of the educational program. The Maple Grove Amish parochial school has built its own horse-drawn "school bus," as the children call it affectionately. It is a buggy with a gray, elongated, boxlike chassis in which twelve girls and two boys ride to school during the week. This conveyance is a concession by the Amish to the distance these "scholars" have to cover. At the same time it economizes on horse power and lessens the danger of crossing busy Lincoln Highway. It is not unusual, however, to see a small stable in the neighborhood of an Amish school. Older boys who live a mile or two away may save time by riding on horseback or in a swift carriage.

The Amish father is patriarch and head of his household and farmstead. To the outsider, his demands on his children may sometimes seem heartless. One Amish farmer, for example, who had been brought to court for "neglecting his daughter's education" by keeping her at home admitted: "I would never have gotten my turkeys to market without her help." But conclusions like that drawn by Principal Ely—"An Amishman wants a large family so that there will be sufficient workers to help with the farm work"[2] are only partly right. Being the patriarch, the Amish father is the highest authority in all matters that affect his family and his farming ventures. His wife and his children to the age of twenty-one are subject to him. Their wages, even if earned within the city, go into the family treasury. In its own inner relationships then, the Amish family has not changed from the old Germanic tradition, of which it was stated in ancient times:

> The blood-related families were the foundation of all private life. As the "prince" stood at the head of the community, of the state, so the father or brother stood as the head of the family, counseling, governing, representing, and protecting. The individual member of the house was not a free agent, but he was a part of an ordered whole with obligations toward the family and from which he could not depart without the consent of the head. . . . Besides the individual will, the will of the family had to be asked and to be listened to.[3]

The general respect and esteem shown to parents and grandparents are at once noticeable. In all community meetings the older men occupy the places of honor. The grandparents spend much of their time visiting their widely scattered relatives and share in all special family events.

Characteristic, furthermore, of Amish family solidarity and cohesiveness is the fact that divisions in the Mennonite church have often occurred along family lines. A limited number of family names may well identify a splinter group. In turn, also, a limited number of family names predominate in certain settlements. The Amish community of east-central Ohio includes only the following names: Anderson, Barkman, Beachy, Bontrager, Bowman, Burkholder, Byler, Chupp, Coblentz, Detweiler, Erb, Frey, Garber, Gingerich, Glick, Helmuth, Hershberger, Hilty, Hochstetler, Kaufman, Keim, Kline, Kuhns, Kurtz, Mast, Miller, Mullet, Nisley, Petersheim, Raber, Schlabach, Schmucker,

Schrock, Shetler, Stutzman, Swartzentruber, Troyer, Weaver, Wengerd, Yoder, Yutzi, and Zook. Three family names —Miller, Yoder, and Troyer—have more baptized members than all the other forty families together. Eight families appear only once: Anderson, Byler, Frey, Glick, Helmuth, Hilty, Petersheim, and Zook.[4]

The high degree of social organization on a family and community basis is maintained to this day. The most effective means of maintaining this control is by "Meidung." Non-conformity, disobedience, or rebellion against the parental authority results, as a rule, in the transgressor's separation or expulsion from the family and the faith, even to his being completely disowned. One Amish father knew neither the whereabouts of his son nor what he was doing after he had left home to make himself free from the father's authority. An Amish mother, although she regretted her son's apostasy, maintained that shunning him was in accordance with the faith. It is worthy of note in this connection that during the last war some Amish boys joined the army instead of serving in Civilian Public Service camps, while in 1960 several Amish youths were given penitentiary sentences for their refusal to fulfil their draft status by serving in some capacity in public institutions. Unique is the case of the Old Order Amish girl who insisted upon acquiring an education. To reconcile her father, who had disowned and disinherited her, she came back to teach in an Amish school not too far from her home.

Although the father has unlimited control over his household, he nevertheless takes his children into his counsel in planning farming matters; particularly does he consider his children's likes and interests. The oldest boy usually has the first claim to a team of horses, the girls milk the cows, and the younger members of the family feed the livestock, heifers, pigs, and chickens. The father works with each child and supervises the work of all until they are of sufficient age and maturity to be intrusted with separate responsibility. The father knows that he cannot raise farmers and succes-

sors if he does not take his children into his confidence, deliberating with them, letting them share in the responsibilities, and yet directing them wisely to the most advantageous programs.

Singular perhaps is the Amish father who was willing to recognize in a daughter a certain artistic urge to paint. He even drove her to the art teacher at the College of Wooster to inquire about the possibilities of taking art courses. But when the family buggy went into a ditch on this trip, the father took the mishap as visible proof that the new undertaking was not blessed by fortune. Time and persistence on the part of the daughter again influenced the father. He permitted her at last to take an expensive correspondence course in painting; he supplied her also with a considerable number of fine-grained crosscut pieces of wood which she used as canvases.

The fair treatment the children receive from father and mother may account for the fact that relatively few seem to try to escape the parental influence: juvenile delinquency is unknown among the Amish. It is true that Amish children perform tasks seemingly too hard for them or at least too hard in the eyes of modern educators. The older Amish do not spare themselves either. They know that life in the country is hard, and, what is more, they make it hard for themselves: their religion tells them it must be hard. As a result, the children, in their physical appearance, are not glowing advertisements for country living. On the other hand, the strenuous life of the whole family seems to be a bond among its members; they want to stay united. Seen in the modern city, the Amish are set off by their calm appearance, their certainty that their mode of life is the right one.

The position of the women in the Amish community is a subordinate one. There are not only many pre-Christian antecedents for this position of the women, but the Christian church seems to give sanction to this Amish custom.

As St. Paul bids the women be silent in church (I Corinthians 6:14), so he commands them also to be subject to their husbands. How could the Apostle speak more plainly than when he said: "Neither was man created for woman, but woman for man" (I Corinthians 11:9). The husband is the God-appointed head and ruler; both wife and children are subject to him. Women and children show this submissiveness, for example, in their attentive silence when an outside visitor is in the home.

One cannot help but notice the small size of the Amish women, who seem drained of strength by too much work in house and barn and by too frequent childbearing. Women's tasks are never done, and their days seem never to end. The tragic effect of this is seen in women prematurely bent and old, in girls who do not attain full stature and growth. The women seem small and rather stunted, squat rather than lithe, in contrast with the heavy stocky figures of the men who seem to grow and develop by the heavy farm work. The women have to help even outdoors, especially in the harvest season. It is not at all unusual to see bonneted girls riding on a hayrake or pitching hay and grain sheaves to the man on the wagon. Nevertheless, the woman may regard herself as fully sharing in her husband's glory only if she cooks, sews, and washes, and rears a large healthy family to help in the enterprise of her husband.

The food on the table, with the exception of bread and butter, the women provide from kitchen, garden, and larder. Quality and substantial amounts are valued over fancy preparation and service. The familiar sight of rows of empty jars stored outside the house or on picket fences gives ample testimony to the women's industry and the appetites of the males.

In their book, *The Family*, sociologists Burgess and Locke gave the Amish family highest ranking on the basis of the following five criteria:

1) The feeling on the part of all members that they belong pre-eminently to the family group and that all other persons are outsiders;
2) the complete integration of individual activities for the achievement of family objectives;
3) the assumption that land, money, and other material goods are family property, involving the obligation to support individual members and give them assistance when they are in need;
4) the willingness of all other members to rally to the support of another member if attacked by outsiders;
5) concern for the perpetuation of the family as evidenced by helping an adult child in beginning and continuing an economic activity in line with family expectations, and in setting up a new household.[5]

These many traits the Amish have brought along from Europe and are trying steadfastly to preserve against the encroaching modern American civilization. Even though settled in a country which proclaims itself the land of the free, it is more and more difficult for them to live independent of the laws and regulations of agencies often unsympathetic and unattentive to their accustomed ways.

STYLES AND COSTUMES

When the Amish went to Broadway a few seasons back in the musical comedy *Plain and Fancy*, no one knows whether it was the "plain" or the "fancy" which attracted wide audiences and made the production a success. Amish costumes certainly lend quaintness to any community, whether on stage or on the streets of real American cities like Wooster, Ohio, Lancaster, Pennsylvania, Goshen, Indiana, or Iowa City, Iowa. The title, "plain people," is, however, a phrase used only in Pennsylvania, never in Ohio. "Plain" clothes simply means solid colors with no furbelows of style. Amish men wear blue, black, or gray work clothes, but their Sunday suits are always blue-black; any Amish in some other color on Sunday is certainly not from central Ohio. The women usually wear dark, somber shades, but in summertime brighter colors also appear in the farm homes of Amishland.

Lapel-less coats with narrow, standing collars and hooks and eyes instead of buttons distinguish the men's clothing from modern styles. Undergarments and trousers have button closings and the "broadfall" or "barndoor"[6] flap instead of vertical or zippered varieties. Younger men prefer to wear blue denim trousers, store-made and standard rather than "western" style. The "broadfall" trousers are usually made in the home. This style of trousers is a carry-over of a fashion from South Germany, where the traditional "Lederhosen" are cut the same way even today.

Belts of leather, which are forbidden in Amish communities, have been troublesome items of discipline over the years. Cloth suspenders are permitted, their width being determined by the bishops. The Amish tolerate rubber only in overshoes and galoshes, but no one knows why rubber suspenders are prohibited, unless as a prevention of exhibitionism. In other Mennonite groups, too, within this section of Ohio, men do not wear belts.

Summer attire often includes sleeveless black vests. Store-purchased shirts, white or blue, now have collars; one may recognize a homemade shirt by its lack of collar, its greater length, and its sewed-up front. Recently sport shirts, modest colored and of wash-and-wear materials, have invaded Amish plain styles. Neckties are another forbidden item, but the men wear a silver or nickel pocket watch on a cloth or leather band—their only extravagance; wrist watches and other jewelry simply are not seen.

Amish beards are as familiar in Ohio as the buggy or the bonnet. When a man comes of marriageable age and has joined the church, he wears a beard. He also shaves his upper and lower lips, and, depending on the ruling of his

61

particular congregation, he may shave his cheeks. The German Landsknecht in the sixteenth and seventeenth centuries shaved his beard but raised instead a mighty moustache as a sign of manliness and bravery. The Amish are believed to have adopted the very opposite practice as a refutation of the value of military prowess and service, but the truth about the origin of the practice is difficult to establish, although it is known that the full beard came into general vogue again during the sixteenth century. Further light is thrown on the Amish style by supposing that the Amish had experiences similar to those of the Old Order Mennonites in Pennsylvania who advised: "The moustache should be shaved above the mouth to avoid offense."[7] The growth on the upper lip had been found obnoxious to congregations when the communion cup was passed, especially when drops were left on the hair. Yet *Ausbund* Hymn 102, Stanza 10, disapproves cutting the hair and beard as opposing God's word. It would seem that aesthetic and religious reasons combine to account for the peculiar style of beard. A scriptural reference demanding the growth of a beard is indeed hard to find.

It is a rare treat for the outsider to find in remote places an old-fashioned blacksmith shop or to watch in some obscure valley the operation of a sawmill tended entirely by men with luxuriant beards and flowing hair; their heads are covered with skullcaps or broadbrimmed hats; heavy aprons cover their loins; broadcloth suspenders hold up heavy, homespun trousers. One wonders whether this is Rip Van Winkle's Catskill country or an "on set" location of an early American frontier film. It is, of course, neither; it is an enclave of a past culture, implanted in the midst of one of America's most populous industrialized states.

"The World's Largest Country Store" in Strasburg, Ohio, owned by Garver Brothers and easily accessible to Amish districts, offers six styles of Amish hats; the number is still not sufficient to supply all the varieties demanded by the men of different districts. The only uniform features about the hats are their black color and the good quality of the felt. In form they vary from a four-inch brim with a four-inch flat crown to three-inch brims with five-inch round crowns. The black band comes in different widths from shoestring size to one inch.

In a gathering of Amishmen, an expert may almost certainly identify members of any particular district by the shape of hat they wear. More and more, though, the variety of hats depends on the indulgence of the manufacturers. For instance, the fine straw hat with flat crown and broad brim formerly favored for summer wear cannot be purchased today. Thus discontinuance of a certain line of material, color, or style forces the Amish to adapt themselves to a previously forbidden item. Any manufactured item used by the Amish may be thus affected. An outstanding example is the caped overcoat formerly worn by the men. Only a few older Amishmen now appear in this garment. Corduroy jackets are becoming almost standard items for cold weather.

The bishop of an Amish district prescribes the length of the men's hair; it may be ordered to be as short as to the upper tip of the ear or as long as to a finger's width below the lobe of an ear. No current hair style may be worn, and combing, parting, and "dressing up" are all forbidden. Patting the hair with the hand, it is believed, will always bring it into order. Amishmen appear without their hats only inside a house, school, or at the Sunday meeting. Most of the men have remarkably healthy looking, vigorous hair.

Although women are the traditional followers of fashion edicts in dress and appearance in mid-century America, in the Amish community the women are even more conservative than the men. The style of the hat and the neckline of the hair of the men allow some variation; the women have no liberty in their coiffures. Their hair is parted in the middle, then brushed back and rolled, never braided, in a knot on the back of the head. All the women wear identical white, net prayer caps and black bonnets.

63

An adult Amish woman never appears without a head covering; in the home this may be a simple piece of cloth; in the Sunday meeting all wear the white prayer caps, which may be tied in a bow under the chin with two long, white ribbons. Unbaptized girls in some districts have to wear the prayer cap in black. A head covering, whatever the form, is now a church ordinance binding for all female members of the entire Mennonite church, regardless of locale or congregational affiliation. No longer is it considered a quaint part of folk costume or as simply an old established custom. St. Paul's verdict in I Corinthians 11:3–5 stands as law:

> But I want you to understand that the head of every man is Christ, the head of a woman is her husband and the head of Christ is God. Any man who prays or prophesies with his head covered dishonors his head [Christ], but any woman who prays or prophesies with her head unveiled dishonors her head [man] [RSV].

With some modern Mennonites the covering is worn only in church, and it assumes forms as different as a black lace shawl and a tiny, round beret-like cap. Every Mennonite congregation demands a uniform style of all women in the group. The Old Order Amish women, however, wear a head covering the entire day. It is obviously more than a "prayer veil," and Joseph M. Yoder contends that it is "more truthfully called subjection veil."[8] The Amish have indeed taken the passage, quoted above, from Paul's First Letter to the Corinthians in a strict interpretation. The woman is in subjection and subordination to her husband, and the head covering is the outward symbol of this fact.

Whether the Amish women have always worn "caps" is not known. The earliest mention of the Dunkards in eastern Holmes County, who may also have been Amish, describes them in this way: "The females are attired in petticoats and short gowns, caps without frills, and when doing outdoor labor, instead of bonnets, wear broad-brimmed

64

hats."[9] The historian, Don Yoder, makes this conjecture: "The little white net cap called the 'prayer veiling' or the prayer covering worn by the women of most plain groups, may be the last surviving American example of the continental German and Swiss peasant 'Haube' or headdress."[10] This authority on the Pennsylvania Amish and Mennonites thinks that this part of the Amish dress, originally part of the European peasant costume, had at first no particular religious significance for the Amish.

Mary Jane Hershey, who has devoted much research to the subject of the head covering, reaches this conclusion:

> Apparently, when women of all churches appeared at public worship with covered heads, there was no specific religious significance attached to the white cap. But when society, in general, changed their headdress, the Mennonite church attempted to maintain the status quo, and consequently, started to teach the importance of women wearing the devotional covering as it is related to the Biblical teaching in I Corinthians 11.[11]

The Amish woman in her large black bonnet shops frequently in small cities like Wooster or Millersburg, Ohio. Modern Mennonite women may also be seen with some kind of abbreviated, tight-fitting headgear; no one mistakes, however, the Old Order Amish lady with her brood of identically bonneted girls and brim-hatted boys. The bonnet identifies the Amish woman; to change the style or black color would invite expulsion from the group. It is interesting to read in Mrs. Hershey's thesis that the "bonnet was not regarded as an essential part of the Mennonite woman's costume during the first half of the nineteenth century."[12] Apparently it was introduced into this country by the Quakers during the last half of the eighteenth century and gradually became associated with plain people; today it is synonymous with Amish style.

The women have freedom in dress only in the choice of

the solid colors of their dresses; the district decides the style in cut, length, and number of pleats. Although black and dark blue predominate, Spector's stores in Walnut Creek and Millersburg, Holmes County, and in Mt. Hope, Wayne County, advertised in the Sugarcreek *Budget* in the summer of 1958: "Summer lawns and Voiles, fine, mercerized, fast color. Pink, Aqua, Orchid, Rose, Maize, Peach, Dark Green, White, Navy, Dark Brown, Dark Wine, Dark Gray, Turquoise and Black. Sale Price, 35 cents per yard." Garver Brothers in Strasburg, Ohio, had a sale of fabrics in these colors: "Oxford (DK) Gray, Medium Deep Brown, Teal Blue, Darkest Copen Blue, Deep Peacock Blue, Bright Navy or Lovely (DK) Plum." Isaac Korsch's mail-order house of Philadelphia advertised in the same issue of the *Budget* "Nicest wash fast summer goods. White, Deep Royal Blue, Soft Dark Gray, Kelly Green, Powder Blue, Lovely Mint Green, Pink, Yellow, Light Green, Natural Tan and Navy."

Prints, flowered materials, stripes, plaids, and mixed colors find no place in Amish styles, and neither does any variation in color of the upper and lower part of the dress or apron. Undergarments may be white, but only the dead are dressed in white otherwise. The total garment of the woman is comparable to that of the Roman Catholic nun of the older orders. The difference is the absence of the wimple and the scapular in the Amish dress, while the veil of the nun has become a shoulder-length hood.

Amish women are always seen wearing an apron, white for the district meetings and the same color as the dress on weekdays. The Sunday apron is a more formal part of the culture. The upper half or "Halstuch" (neckcloth) begins with a point in the middle of the back, ascends then in V-shape over the shoulders, is tucked into the high neckline of the dress, and falls doubled across the chest into the band of the lower apron. Straight pins hold the full-length lower part of the apron in place. Small children often wear an apron which is a full-dress style, extending from the neck to the ankles and forearm, but open in the back; the upper part is closed with four buttons.

In wintertime the women wear a full scarf or shawl of black, heavy wool which extends over much of the back. The bonnet in bitter weather may also be more substantial; stockings are black lisle. Some years ago button shoes were as necessary as bonnets; no other style appeared. Today, however, button shoes have disappeared from the manufacturers' inventories and are no longer available. Women now substitute black oxfords with medium-size heels. The shoes are another example of adaptation by the Amish; when the preferred style of shoe was no longer available, the women simply had to substitute more modern footwear. It is likely that, before this happened, all buttoned shoes available in manufacturers' supplies had been exhausted.

The dresses of the women are closed with clasps or simple straight pins rather than buttons; only the smaller children's garments have buttoned closings on the back. The little Amish girl, often a replica of her mother in bonnet, dress, and shoes is a rare treat to observe; her shyness and reserve make it impossible to do more than smile and observe her from afar. Even the small babies are dressed as much as possible in Amish costume; the sight of an entire family—father, mother, a half-dozen children and infants all crowded into a buggy on a warm Sunday morning—is one of the pleasant observations in Wayne and Holmes counties today.

There are still a few Amish districts in which the women wear a two-piece dress not unlike the Alpine blouse and bodice with its full skirt; in Ohio, skirt and blouse are always of the same color, and the bodice is not laced or hooked in front.

Hair "fancying" is unknown to the adult Amish woman; she neither bobs, curls, nor braids her hair. The young girls do braid but do not allow the hair to hang from their heads. Women wear no jewelry or wedding rings, nor do the men. The wrath of the Old Testament prophets, Isaiah (chap.

3) and Jeremiah (chap. 4), is too strong to be misunderstood in this respect; the approval of St. Paul (I Timothy 2:9; I Corinthians 11:15) and St. Peter (I Peter 3:3) would be withdrawn if any showy items were worn. Nothing should accentuate, enhance, or adorn the female figure, according to Amish law.

The purchases from the autumn trip to Garver Brothers "Country Store" or similar Amish trading places keep the womenfolk busy during the long winter months. They buy cotton, muslin, net, denim, and corduroy goods in bales; hooks, eyes, and small dark buttons by the gross. The women plan these shopping forays carefully, timing them so that good quality materials at reasonable prices may be secured. Large families need ample supplies of clothing; perhaps a trousseau must be planned for a marriageable daughter. The trip is reminiscent, in reverse, of the visit of the peddler to pioneer families along the frontier pike.

Changes in costume and style do occur, but they become apparent only over an extended period of time. As suggested before, the Amish are dependent on manufacturers more than they may like to be. Nevertheless no sudden whim or fancy would bring about change in Amish styles; caprice plays no part in Amish progress. But while style is rigid, the observer who has watched these people over a number of years must concede that their mode of living undergoes a slow, progressive change. Mrs. Hershey is right when she remarks that the tradition-conscious Mennonites in the United States "have confused a static culture with non-conformity,"[13] but that culture is nevertheless in a state of flux. The Amish have not made models of their forebears; they have no museum pieces to which they may refer; they do not keep detailed minutes of the bishops' regulations. Slow changes in dress and general appearance have occurred since the time of Jakob Ammann in 1693. Deviations develop from existing patterns; nothing is totally an innovation; no gaps and no leaps appear. Non-avail-

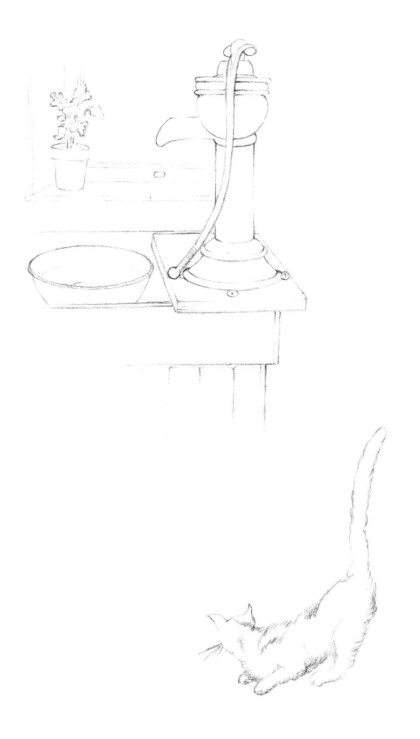

ability forces the Amish to adapt themselves to different items, in clothing as well as in equipment.

Practical, rugged ways of living also influence the styles of the Amish. Bright, fragile colors or delicate materials would be impractical in their simple farm life. Deprived by biblical edict of the dubious privilege of wearing slacks, shorts, or trousers, the Amish woman dons her voluminous dark skirt to milk the cows, to help her husband in the field, to climb into a narrow surrey and to ride out in weather, fair or stormy. She believes the purposes of dress and headgear are warmth and protection. She likes her long dress and the three-quarter length sleeve, as well as her bonnet and her serviceable shoes. Her social problems are not complex; she seems to live without outward exhibition, free from competition in dress with her Amish sisters. She may compete in canning prowess or other culinary skills with other women, but status-seeking in Amishland is not pursued by style or cosmetics.

The Amish costume is not modern, but it is dignified and picturesque. American fashions may never return to the Amish styles, but edicts from Paris, Fifth Avenue, or high-pressure salons and couturiers must stop at the entrance to the country lane. These Amish women, perhaps unconsciously, reveal the past to present-day America; undoubtedly it is the ankle- or calf-length costumes of the women and the severe suits of the men which continually invite comment and excite curiosity about these people among city dwellers.

When Calvin George Bachmann says that "the Amish seek to show that they are not of this world with its changing fashions; that they are concerned, not with the outward which alone man sees, but with the inward, which is seen alone by God,"[14] he seems to say that the Amish consciously created their present style of clothing. This is not so. Their present mode of dressing is evidence of the cultural lag which is characteristic of the total picture of Amish life.

During their days of repression they dared not set themselves off by outward display; they had to conform to and blend with the surrounding culture. But in America, where change in personal appearance has been so rapid and noticeable through the cheap mechanical multiplication of styles, the Amish have resisted the quick upheaval, thereby preserving essentially a picture of early nineteenth-century pioneer days.

CHAPTER III

THE OLD ORDER AMISH
WAY OF LIFE

WORLDLY WAYS AND PECULIARITIES

The Amish are a people of seclusion. By intent and tradition they live withdrawn from the concourse of the world. They have not gone forth to reform American ways; on the contrary, it has been their tenacity in holding still that has provoked conflict with modern society. Mainly as a result of such clashes has attention at times been called to the Amish way of life.

It is with the most conservative element within Amish society, solidly welded to its traditional behavior, that the ever-widening and penetrating American culture comes to wrestle. The "Meidung" case in Wayne County in 1947 (see chap. iv) and the "Social Security Tax" case in 1958 (see chap. i) are recent and pronounced examples of conflicts that have provoked widespread attention. As far as the Amish are concerned, these and similar unhappy situations are forced upon them; as usual, their defenses were determinedly passive and almost totally negative.

There are inconsistencies, one observes, in the Amish adaptation to modern America: for instance, when they were taken to court over their boycott of a man for possessing an automobile, the defendants themselves hired a car to come to the trial; again, they have themselves underwritten a private bus line which runs conveniently through their territory, but they do not permit one of their own group to be a driver; and, although they use tractors for belt-power to thresh and grind feed for their cattle, they themselves cannot use the tractor for plowing. In another paradoxical instance an enterprising young Amishman built a planing mill but, since electricity is forbidden, he installed a diesel motor to provide power; at the same time many Amish use the electricity, light, and telephone facilities in farmhouses acquired by mortgage, yet would never instal these by themselves; some use gasoline for Mortland lamps or for motors to power spray guns to paint their barns but draw the line against gasoline as a motor transport fuel. Nevertheless, in spite of these inconsistencies, there is the inescapable fact of Amish unity that manifests itself in the identical appearance of all adult male Amishmen, in the somber colors of all hooded women, in the children, diminutive replicas of their elders, and in the peaceful scene of husband and wife as they ride along the country road in their frail, square-boxed, black surrey.

One wonders how it is possible that a distinctive group of people can stand aside here in the heart of modern America, a country ostensibly at the peak of Western culture, and yet outwardly have no part of it. What gives them the strength to resist the seemingly irresistible conveniences, the automobile, the tractor, electricity, refrigeration, radio, central heating, hot and cold running water in the home? It is not a lack of mental alacrity, as some critics assert, for these are shrewd and alert people. Nor can it be cupidity or the lust for hard cash, of which they are frequently accused, for the Amish are as generous and charitable as any group of farmers; Freedom Train, CROP, and various foreign relief projects have proven this sufficiently. Furthermore, their farms, and particularly their houses and barns, fences, front lawns and gardens, their livestock and their horses are models for anyone interested in rural activity.

Fundamental for all Mennonite bodies, including the Amish, is the content of the Schleitheim Confession of Faith of 1527 and the later Dortrecht Confession of Faith of 1632, both of which focus on these points: voluntary membership, with adult baptism as symbol of that membership; refusal to bear arms and to participate in government whether local or national; communion and footwashing among members of the group; rejection of the oath; separation from non-believers; the expulsion of the unfaithful, but extensive mutual aid among all faithful members; the ordination of leaders of the local group. Obviously, the Amish way of life cannot be explained solely on the basis of these doctrines. Progressive Mennonite groups, too, base themselves on these tenets. While this writer does not seek to disclaim or belittle the religious impetus in the origin of the Anabaptist group, he must nevertheless differentiate between the strictly confessional and ritual elements of the Old Order Amish sect and the external accouterments which have accumulated only in America.

The Amish themselves place the focus of the argument of differentiation between themselves and every other group upon one word, *world*. Every unadopted and unacceptable item of contemporary culture is decried as "worldly." *World* has come to be synonymous with *city*, with which the Amish identify all evil, as with Sodom and Gomorrah in Lot's time. The "world," the city, has meant for him in the past the enemy, the persecutor and suppressor of his religious life as well as his culture. Mistrusting and avoiding the "world," the Amish identify with the country; their faith lends sanctity to the rural habitat.

To inquire now, as a test for Amish integrity, for the true

meaning of the concept of "world" as the New Testament writers used it is fruitless. Still in all sincerity and objectivity one may ask, for example, where one would find a biblical prohibition against buttons on all outer garments but no prohibition against them on trousers and undergarments? Or where are the biblical references that enjoin buttons on the man's trousers and shirt but hooks and eyes for his coat? Or where would one find a prescription for fifteen straight pins on a woman's dress, but precisely four buttons on the upper back of a child's garment? Reasons of safety aside, what was the practice in apostolic times? Where is the justification for the bearded growth around a man's chin and cheek, but not on his upper and lower lip? Or for permission to wear rubber overshoes but condemnation for the use of rubber in the man's suspenders or anywhere else on the human person?

Characteristically the Amish use the Bible both positively and negatively. The Apostle says, for instance, "Be ye separate." The Amish take this to mean that they must live in the country. One could add here that it has come to mean rather to "die" in the country, because Amish do come to work in the city and, of course, they carry on commerce with the "world" and expect to make a good livelihood from it. At all events they hope to remove later in life back to the country. On the other hand, to the Amish argument that, since tractor and electricity are not mentioned in the Bible, they are not meant for human employment, one could easily reply that ice cream, bottled gas for cooking and refrigeration, and canned goods so conveniently bought at the crossroads grocery store are also not mentioned. But the passages they have selected and the interpretations they have given them have come to mean a way of life to these people. Obedience to the rule assures salvation. To the outsider these biblical quotes seem, if not an escape, at least a defense against those particular modern achievements which the Amish have not found it feasible to adopt.

Attention must be called to the fact that negativism toward possession does not at all imply stubborn abhorrence or inconoclasm. Strangely enough, the sectarian taboo affects only ownership, not use. Such equivocal behavior perplexes the average American. The most glaring example, as already mentioned, is that of the Amish defendants in the "Meidung" trial who ostracized a man for possessing an automobile but themselves came and left the courthouse in a hired automobile. Just as provocative is the case of the young unbaptized Amishman who owns an automobile and a tractor for field work. He not only provides transportation for his numerous family and neighbors but also works his father's large farm and many of his neighbors'. He has been able to defer baptism and official group membership and prefers to postpone these as long as his group will tolerate his doing so because he will have to give up the mechanical possessions upon baptism. A still more striking example is the Lentus Bus Line which was underwritten by thirty Amish families and whose signatures, with an investment of $9,000, assured the establishment of a bus route used almost exclusively by the Amish. The bus line does not operate on Sunday or Wednesday afternoon, when most stores in the city of Wooster are closed.

American economic forces have molded the Amish more than they themselves perhaps would be willing to admit. Until a few years ago high button shoes for the women were the standard, uncompromised, footgear. Today, however, they cannot be bought anywhere in America. They have completely disappeared, and the Amish do not manufacture their own shoes. Thus, high button shoes are no longer required. A similar change is affecting the men's black felt and round summer hats which have become entirely dependent on the co-operation of manufacturers rather than on the bishops' prescriptions. Consider, too, that the Amish have accepted the buggy as a proper vehicle, although it came into use only fifty to seventy years ago, and they have accepted the steel plow and such other

modern manufactured agricultural implements as the cultivator, reaper, cutter, threshing machine, manure spreader, disk harrow, and the like. It is necessary to add, however, that the Amish are pressed to these adoptions because manufacturers are no longer producing horse-drawn equipment. Such tools, therefore, are at a premium at any sale or auction and sometimes bring double and triple cost price.

On the other hand, standard American equipment, such as central heating and running hot and cold water systems, seem wasteful to the thrifty Amish. This curious selectivity results in interesting combinations of older and newer methods of operation. One enterprising younger Amishman plants, cultivates, and digs potatoes with teams of horses. That same Amish entrepreneur uses a gasoline motor to pull the loaded harvest wagon backward into the upper story of the barn, to hoist the load into the bin, and finally to work his modern grading machinery. In addition he uses the latest mechanical gadget to close the paper bags.

In their professed zeal to model their lives after that of the Apostles, the Old Order Amish seem to have lost sight of the fact that the Apostles nonetheless lived in the same manner as their contemporary society, at least without notable difference in outward appearance from others in the Roman communities. Similarly, in the sixteenth century the progenitors of the Anabaptist persuasion were sought out and subjected to fire and sword for their nonconformity in belief, not in outward guise. Deviation from prevailing culture patterns, as exhibited in Wayne and Holmes counties today, would have been impossible during that age of persecution. One might wish that some Amishman might have a chance to go back to that time and see for himself and then to come and report on his findings, as one of the group did concerning the roundness of the earth. To settle the argument of whether the earth is round or flat, one local Amishman took off on a round-the-world cruise to find out whether it could be done. He left with two suits, one black and a white one specially made for the journey; he returned with but one. The black one had been taken from him along the way. Nevertheless he proved to his own satisfaction and that of most of his neighbors that the earth is not flat, as they had always been led to believe.

The attempt to understand the Amish and to penetrate their mode of living must lead in two directions. The first must lead to religion, because the Amish claim in all disputes and clashes with the surrounding culture a scriptural basis for their position. It is necessary to see what scriptural passages they claim for themselves and to scrutinize the soundness of their position. The second must consider the setting in which the Amish are found, the rural agricultural environment which is synonymous with the Amish way of life.

Scriptural Basis

Preacher Eli J. Miller, who died in 1946 at the age of 74, enjoyed unusual respect and authority within the whole Old Order Amish settlement. He represented the ideal Amish combination of religious and farming achievement. Not only was he a popular speaker, capable of attracting a great following whenever he appeared, but he advanced his own private holdings from a small rented farmstead to a 160-acre farm which he owned and which could be exhibited as a model for all his fellow sectarians. During his lifetime, prosperity characterized the whole community, and strife and dissension were often cleared by his wise judgment. Eli Miller could speak with authority for his people. It was to Preacher Miller that the author turned for a reliable account of the scriptural passages underlying the Amish way of life and faith.

The following summary of the scriptural references undergirding the Amish way of life and belief is based on a conversation held with Preacher Miller in December, 1944, at his farm home east of Wooster. His remarks constituted as sincere and honest a statement of Amish doctrine as the author has ever heard. Preacher Miller gave carefully considered answers to the questions put him. The biblical texts (King James Version, Standard Edition) and the brief explanations incorporated in the following summary are a direct result of this interview. They are given to help clarify Amish faith but of course do not supplant the formal Confession of Faith.

Adult Baptism

(As the distinguishing mark of the Anabaptist Christian Church.) Acts 2:38: Repent ye, and be baptized. (The inclusion of "Repent ye" is intended to exclude baptism of children who cannot have repented before they are baptized.)

Refusal To Bear Arms

(Hunting with firearms is not included in these proscriptions.) Matthew 5:38: Ye have heard that it was said, An eye for an eye, and a tooth for a tooth: 39: but I say unto you, Resist not him that is evil: but whosoever smiteth thee on the right cheek, turn to him the other also. 40: And if any man would go to law with thee, and take away thy coat, let him have thy cloak also. 41: And whosoever shall compel thee to go one mile, go with him two. 42: Give to him that asketh thee, and from him that would borrow of thee turn not thou away. 43: Ye have heard that it was said, Thou shalt love thy neighbor, and hate thine enemy: 44: but I say unto you, Love your enemies, and pray for them that persecute you; 45: that ye may be sons of your Father who is in heaven: for he maketh his sun to rise on the evil and the good and sendeth rain on the just and the unjust. Romans 12:17: Render to no man evil for evil. Take thought for things honorable in the sight of all men. 18: If it be possible, as much as in you lieth, be at peace with all men. 19: Avenge not yourselves, beloved, but give place unto the wrath of God: for it is written, Vengeance belongeth unto me: I will recompense, saith the Lord. 20: But if thine enemy hunger, feed him; if he thirst, give him to drink; for in so doing thou shalt heap coals of fire upon his head. 21: Be not overcome of evil, but overcome evil with good. II Corinthians 10:4: For weapons of our warfare are not of the flesh, but mighty before God to the casting down of strongholds. II Timothy 2:24: And the Lord's servant must not strive, but be gentle towards all, apt to teach, forbearing. Hebrews 12:14: Follow after peace with all men, and the sanctification without which no man shall see the Lord. (Edwin Mills, sheriff of Wayne County, 1937–48, related this outstanding incident which occurred during his term of office: Many head of cattle had been stolen from an Amish farm and then sold. The Amishman refused to accept the money which the sheriff recovered, nor did he consent to prosecute the culprits.)

The Separation of the Church from the World

(For the Amishman this implies nonconformity in dress, in personal appointment, in home and farm conveniences, in amusements—in any external item the Amish have come to understand under the general term "world.") John 17: 14: I have given them thy word; and the world hated them, because they are not of the world, even as I am not of the world. . . . 16: They are not of the world, even as I am not of the world. II Corinthians 6:14: Be not unequally yoked with unbelievers: for what fellowship have righteousness and iniquity? or what communion hath light with darkness? 15: And what concord hath Christ with Belial? or what portion hath a believer with an unbeliever? 16: And what agreement hath a temple of God with idols? for we are a temple of the living God; even as God said, I will dwell in them, and walk in them; and I will be their God, and they shall be my people. 17: Wherefore: Come ye out from among them and be ye separate, saith the Lord, And touch no unclean thing; And I will receive you, 18: And will be to you a Father, And ye shall be to me sons and daughters, saith the Lord Almighty. James 1:27: Pure religion and undefiled before our God and Father is this . . . to keep oneself unspotted from the world. James 4:4: Ye adulteresses, know ye not that the friendship of the world is enmity with God? Whosoever therefore would be a friend of the world maketh himself an enemy of God. I Peter 2:9: But ye are an elect race, a royal priesthood, a holy nation, a people for God's own possession, that ye may show forth the excellencies of him who called you out of darkness into his marvelous light. . . . I John 2:15: Love not the world, neither the things that are in the world. If any man love the world, the love of the Father is not in him. (Nonconformity in dress is emphasized.) Romans 12:2: And be not fashioned according to the world. I Peter 1:13: Girding up the loins . . . 14: as children of obedience, not fashioning yourselves according to your former lusts in time of your ignorance. (Dress must be substantial.) Genesis 3:7: . . . and they sewed fig-leaves together, and made themselves aprons. 21: And Jehovah God made for Adam and for his wife coats of skins, and clothed them. (Dress must be modest.) I Timothy 2:9: In like manner, that women adorn themselves in modest apparel, with shamefastness and sobriety; not with braided hair, and gold or pearls or costly raiment. I Peter 3:3: Whose adorning let it not be the outward adorning of braiding the hair, and of wearing jewels of gold, or of putting on apparel; 4: but let it be the hidden man of the heart. (Dress must be economical.) I Timothy 2:9: (as above); I Peter 3:3: (as above). (Dress must be appropriate to sex.) Deuteronomy 22:5: A woman shall not wear that which pertaineth unto a man, neither shall a man put on a woman's garment. (Dress must include no jewelry or ornamentation.) Isaiah 3:16: Moreover Jehovah said, Because the daughters of Zion are haughty, and walk with outstretched necks and wanton eyes, walking and mincing as they go, and making a tinkling with

their feet; 17: therefore the Lord will smite with a scab the crown of the head of the daughters of Zion, and Jehovah will lay bare their secret parts. 18: In that day the Lord will take away the beauty of their anklets, and the cauls, and the crescents; 19: the pendants, and the bracelets, and the mufflers; 20: the headtires, and the ankle chains, and the sashes, and the perfume-boxes, and the amulets; 21: the rings and the nose-jewels; 22: the festival robes, and the mantles, and the shawls, and the satchels; 23: the hand-mirrors, and the fine linen, and the turbans, and the veils. 24: And it shall come to pass, that instead of sweet spices there shall be rottenness; and instead of a girdle, a rope; and instead of well set hair, baldness; and instead of a robe, a girding of sackcloth; branding instead of beauty.

Pride

(This is the cardinal and all-inclusive sin for the Amish. To depart from the inherited or accustomed order or style in dress, haircut, wagons, buggies, or various other customs is to commit it.) Luke 9:23: If any man would come after me, let him deny himself, and take up his cross daily, and follow me. Philippians 2:5: Have this mind in you, which was also in Christ Jesus: 6: who, existing in the form of God, counted not the being on an equality with God a thing to be grasped; 7: but emptied himself, taking the form of a servant, being made in the likeness of men; 8: and being found in fashion as a man, he humbled himself, becoming obedient even unto death, yea, the death of the cross. 9: Wherefore also God highly exalted him, and gave unto him the name which is above every name; 10: that in the name of Jesus every knee should bow, of things in heaven and things on earth and things under the earth; 11: and that every tongue should confess that Jesus Christ is Lord, to the glory of God the Father. I Peter 5:5: Like-wise, ye younger, be subject unto the elder. . . . 6: Humble yourselves therefore under the mighty hand of God, that he may exalt you in due time. I Corinthians 11:1: Be ye imitators of me, even as I also am of Christ. 2: Now I praise you that ye remember me in all things, and hold fast the traditions, even as I delivered them to you. 3: But I would have you know, that the head of every man is Christ; and the head of the woman is the man; and the head of Christ is God. 4: Every man praying or prophesying, having his head covered, dishonoreth his head. 5: But every woman praying or prophesying with her head unveiled dishonoreth her head; for it is one and the same thing as if she were shaven. (This explains the Amish woman's traditional head covering.) 6: For if a woman is not veiled, let her also be shorn; but if it is a shame to a woman to be shorn or shaven, let her be veiled. 7: For a man indeed ought not to have his head veiled, forasmuch as he is the image and glory of God: but the woman is the glory of the man. 8: For the man is not of the woman; but the woman of the man: 9: for neither was the man created for the woman; but the woman for the man: 10: for this cause ought the woman to have a sign of authority on her head, because of the angels. 11: Nevertheless, neither is the woman without the man, nor the man without the woman, in the Lord. 12: For as the woman is of the man, so is the man also by the woman; but all things are of God. 13: Judge ye in yourselves: is it seemly that a woman pray unto God unveiled? 14: Doth not even nature itself teach you, that, if a man have long hair, it is a dishonor to him? 15: But if a woman have long hair, it is a glory to her: for her hair is given her for a covering. 16: But if any man seemeth to be contentious, we have no such custom, neither the churches of God. (Amish women do use comb and hair brush, but their hair is neither cut short, curled, nor braided. The hair is rolled and pinned in the back under the prayer cap. Only the smaller girls have their hair braided. Sometimes the merest semblance of a mirror may be seen in the home.)

Avoidance of Organizations

(This includes life insurance, political organizations, secret societies, clubs of every sort, and farm organizations.) II Corinthians 6:14: Be not unequally yoked with unbelievers: for what fellowship have righteousness and iniquity? or what communion hath light with darkness? (The only notable exception seems to be Alcoholics Anonymous. Several Wayne and Holmes County Amishmen and their wives are regular attendants at the Wooster, Fredericksburg, and Millersburg meetings. A few of them do even lead and speak of their deliverance from alcohol at meetings throughout the state. In fact, special "Amish nights" are occasionally held by distant A.A. groups.)

Church Discipline

(This includes such matters as the parting and cutting of men's hair, the painting of buggies, and other details of life and activities.) Ephesians 4:1: I therefore, the prisoner in the Lord, beseech you to walk worthily of the calling wherewith ye were called, 2: with all lowliness and meekness, with long-suffering, forbearing one another in love. I John 1:7: But if we walk in the light, as he is in the light, we have fellowship one with another, and the blood of Jesus his Son cleanseth us from all sin. Colossians 3:23: Whatsoever ye do, work heartily.

The Choosing of Bishops and Ministers, Deacons

Acts 1:24: And they prayed, and said, Thou, Lord, who knowest the hearts of all men, show of these two the one whom thou hast chosen, 25: to take the place in this ministry and apostleship from which Judas fell away, that he might go to his own place. 26: And they gave lots for them; and the lot fell upon Mathias and he was numbered with the eleven apostles.

85

On Pictures, Photographs and Mirrors

Exodus 20:4: Thou shalt not make unto thee a graven image, nor any likeness of any thing that is in heaven above, or that is in the earth beneath, or that is in the water under the earth.

Examining the biblical references given by Preacher Miller, one may see a justification for the fundamental doctrines of the Anabaptist faith. The New Testament writers, definite in their demand for separation from the world, set a limit, for example, to the female propensity toward showiness in externals.

There is no doubt that the Bible is a source of strength and comfort to the Amish. More time is given to its reading in the Sunday gathering of the Gemei than in other Protestant services. Moreover, "es steht geschrieben" ("it stands written") is final, authoritative, and decisive in all disputes among the Amish. Contesting "the Word" breaks the pillars of Amish strength and purpose. Still, the Old Order Amish do not read the Bible at random but rather select for emphasis and interpretation those chapters which are suitable to their needs and ways.

A critical reader of the Scriptures, however, will fail to find any basis for the minutiae of dress and behavior which characterize the American Old Order Amish. The cuffs and the broadfall of a man's trousers, the lapel, the hooks and eyes, the flap of a pocket of a man's coat, the color, brim, and crown of a man's hat do not have explicit biblical sanction. The pleats, the hem, the waistband, cut of neck, the straight pins, the length of the sleeve of the woman's dress —all these, so exactly ordered now, are nowhere mentioned in the Bible.

The careful observer must conclude that Amish taboos are directed mainly against such elements of modern culture which might form entering wedges that would sooner or later cleave their rural society asunder. Thus, though corn planters and manure spreaders are just as modern as the automobile and telephone, they do not disrupt agricultural life; nor do they offer a chance to escape to the worldly city. Whatever the contribution of city culture—automobile, electricity, factory-made clothes or hair style—if it might lure an Amishman to change his abode, it is taboo.

In describing the Old Order Amish, religious faith and beliefs must be given the chief places, but they cannot be regarded as the total explanation for a mode of life which in its justification, salvation, and orthodoxy makes itself dependent on infinitesimal details of appearance and behavior. One doubts whether Scripture can be held to account for ostracizing, shunning, or boycotting a neighbor or community of neighbors who digress from a group pattern, such as, for example, the permissible length for the bobbing of hair.

Is religious indignation a legitimate excuse for the break in relations with an otherwise industrious, devout farmer who purchases a family conveyance with a three-inch-square glass window in the side of the curtain? Do matters like this signify a man's Christianity? A kerosene lamp or an extra reflector on the back part of the horse-drawn carriage seem too superficial as criteria of brotherly love. To equate such trifles with neighborliness, Christian charity, and helpfulness seems somehow to negate true religion. Why do Old Testament literalism and legalism find such strong support in the daily life of the Amish? Other factors beside scriptural injunction must lie beneath these Old Order Amish peculiarities. The following section attempts to discover them.

EUROPEAN RURAL SOCIETY TRANSPLANTED TO AMERICA

Old Order Amish Bishop Roman Troyer intimated the possible reason for his peoples' ways when he stated in vigorous German, "Ich bin ein Bauer. Wir sind Bauern" ("I am a peasant. We are peasants"). Here is a clue to help explain Amish mores.

The bishop's statement suggests the strong connection between the Amish as a religious group and their attachment to a rural life. Perhaps it is because they succeeded in re-establishing their peasant community in America that the Amish have been able to resist the "melting pot" philosophy and to maintain their own identity. For the structure of their peasant or rural ways helps them preserve their spiritual unity, while religious and rural traditions have become intertwined and almost interdependent. I have already considered the religious nature of the Amish at some length. Evidence to support and explain the "Bauer" viewpoint will be presented here.

As a person of European background from original peasant stock, this writer sees a remarkable similarity between the "Bauern" of western Germany and the Amish of rural Ohio. They think alike; they have similar physical characteristics; both are isolated in their geographic setting; their religious convictions are both fundamentalist, and their outlook on life is conservative. A respected, thorough student of Mennonite and Amish history, John Umble, corroborates this interpretation of the Amish as a peasant group in his statement:

> Through persecution and martyrdom they [i.e., the Amish] lost their educated leadership during the first half century following their organization in 1525, and became a peasant group, driven from land to land for their refusal to conform to the established order. . . . Restrictions (i.e. on marriage, residence, property, religious services, ordination of ministers) still further confined the group within the peasant status. This peasant tradition the Amish brought with them to colonial Pennsylvania and are maintaining it with a surprising degree of success. Hence the Old Order Amish of twentieth century America furnish first hand mate-

rial for studying a certain type of sixteenth century German peasant life.[1]

Umble goes on to say that the progenitors of the Amish lost their missionary zeal and aggressiveness through the vehemence of persecution and that they came eventually not only to accept their peasant status but to adopt the conviction "that the peasant status alone afforded the proper environment for living an acceptable Christian life."[2] John Umble's conclusion regarding the Amish reads in part:

> The Amish preserved a simple sixteenth century German peasant tradition in the midst of our complex American society. In dress, in manners, in folk ways, in language, in forms of religious worship, they still preserve the tradition of the better type of Christian peasant farmer of the German Palatinate, of Alsace-Lorraine, and of colonial Pennsylvania.[3]

During the last half century, particularly after the National Socialist regime proclaimed that the whole German state was to be founded on a new concept of "Bauerntum," "peasantry," much thought and study have been directed toward the German "Bauer." Under Hitler, peasantry was glorified anew as the first profession of the nation from which all culture took its origin. Soil and nature combined to rear the rural inhabitant, so it was said, and from him was to come the regeneration of twentieth-century civilization. The "Bauer" was acclaimed as "the eternal man." Writers of the blood-and-soil philosophy went to great lengths to extol the innocence or primitive stage of development of the "Bauer." Older students of cultural history had also called attention to this solid kernel of the populace, secure against crisis, fountainhead of civilization, the original base of a nation, from which new stock could always arise.

The pressure of the past, and especially of the Middle

Ages, has indeed created an infinite toughness in the German "Bauer"; no group in society has been subjected to such hardship, torment, enslavement, and persecution. Peasant wisdom substantiates this idea of durable strength, as in the saying: "Leg dich krumm, so hilft dir Gott" ("lay yourself . . . bend yourself," i.e., fit yourself into the situation, and God will help you). This conservatism of the European peasant is still a vast power, which despite surrounding change remains a firm, enduring influence in his society. And the conservatism of the "Bauer" is largely a matter of custom, which he reveres. Similarly, the Amish have formed a dam of conservatism from their earliest beginnings. Both in Europe and America the Amish have proceeded from custom, tradition, sense of family and community. At the same time, the "Bauer," now including the Amishman, is a practical man, aiming at practical results. He is not interested in words for words' sake. He works purposefully and soberly to till his fields, his mind far removed from scholarly systems of philosophy or theology.

In practical ways the "Bauer" in the Amishland adheres rigidly to old accustomed ways in ordering his life. He does not begin to plant corn until the leaves of the white oak are the size of a squirrel's paw. He does not begin to harvest during the weekend. He cleans his chicken house when the moon is in a desired phase. He usually does not court or marry in spring or summer, but rather in fall or winter. He marries on Tuesday or Thursday, and often the astral signs of the calendar seem to be more important to him than the actual dates. Fixed customs govern his life and duties in home, barn, and field. They seem to control his dress, habits of eating and drinking, recreation, society with friends; in short, almost every step from birth to death is ordained. One recalls the distinction between "peasant" and "farmer" made by a progressive Mennonite. Himself he considered a "farmer," a capitalist relying on a local bank, related social agencies, modern industrial products and equipment, fertilizer, modern methods, and technology. The "peasant," however, depended not at all on modern implements or techniques but relied in great part on signs of the zodiac, phases of the moon and stars, the clouds in the sky, and the flight of the swallows, on his ancestors' teaching and edicts, on customs and traditions known to him since birth.

For the Amish, untutored and hostile in many ways to formal learning, religion is not so much a matter of theological dogma as of the literal adherence to the commands of Scripture, as handed down from generation to generation. Without deprecating their spiritual beliefs or unity, one could suggest that religion and custom or mores have become one for the Amish. Fundamentalist religion with Old Testament rigidity rules their lives much more than does the religion of outreach of liberal Protestantism govern the behavior of its adherents. Custom and tradition dictate the Amish way of life just as they do that of the European peasant. The Amish district is the guardian of tradition, its elected overseers are the administrators of tradition. Tradition guards against chaos, which results when new ideas or changes in outer appearance or costume seek to invade Amish life. The ways of the ancestors, expressed by the statement, "That's the way our fathers did it, and that's the way we do it," may be heard repeatedly in Amishland. This rule is honored and followed and only rarely examined or challenged. Customs are good because they are old, and authentic for the same reason. How they came into existence is of secondary importance; they are hallowed by time. Out of touch with new ideas and ways, the Amish want no change in their mores, and therefore utterly insignificant items are often magnified into issues that divide a community. A curl in the hair or the possession of a wedding ring have been subjects of intense dispute. Still, many Amish accept the hard rule of custom and tradition and live comfortably in its grasp. It is one with their religious beliefs and with their daily routine. But many critical members of the Ohio Amish community, and especially younger members, find custom a tormenting barrier.

As has been mentioned, the greatest sin for the Amish is pride, and pride means rebellion against the customs of the group. This sin, if not confessed before the district and atoned, is punishable with anathema, casting out, "Meidung"—death as far as the community is concerned. One might conclude from this that the mores of the group are its highest good.

Similarly, in *Meier Helmbrecht*, the oldest thirteenth-century German document about farm life, the father admonishes his wayward son:

> Schlag die Hof-fahrt Dir aus dem Sinn
> Lass selband uns wacker
> Bestellen den Acker.
> So steigst gleich mir Du hinab
> Mit grossen Ehren in Dein Grab.[4]

> ("Rid yourself of pride.
> Let us both busily
> plow our field.
> Then you as I will with great honor
> descend to the grave" [my translation].)

These words might well have been spoken this very day in east-central Ohio.

It is an incontestable Amish inheritance to recognize a heaven above, an earth below, and the obligation to perform the daily chores on the farm. It is also the acknowledged destiny of the Amish to be placed between heaven and earth in order to unify the two in their daily life. The Old Order Amishman feels himself encompassed by the growth of nature and fitted into its eternal law. God and nature are inseparable; God, life, family, soil, farm, weather, district form one unbroken unity. Generations come, but the labor remains the same, just as do the changes in the seasons, sowing and reaping, day and night. This unity is the founda-

tion of the Amish way of life. To live, grow, and pass on the tradition is his road, while above beckons the eternal God. Every member of the group tries to adjust to this in the manner peculiar to the Amish and to allow nothing to destroy the essential qualities of this make-up.

The Amish regard their manners and customs, their everyday life, as synonymous with religion, as God-ordained, as the road to salvation. To question the rightness of these customs is equivalent to denying the very nature of religion. Only the agencies of the state and the outside world can be questioned. When the latter try to mold and reshape Amish mores, religious sanction, so say the Amish, is on their side. The Amish, through their bishops, have at times opposed the rulings of the state. For instance, during the winter and spring of 1960–61 several men and one woman accepted five-day jail terms for failure, in compliance with the command of their bishops, to provide proper lighting on their buggies. The state was unrelenting, and later the Amish were obliged to modify their mores.

The Amish, of course, consider that the state unduly invades their society. Recurrent and ever-renewed examples flare up in connection with the education of the children. The state, for example, has not only attempted to abolish the one-room school but has repeatedly raised the school attendance age which, at the present writing in 1961, is sixteen. The Amish claim that they had developed their group life in east-central Ohio before the state came to infringe upon their enclave with compulsory education. Thus, encroachments upon the rural isolation are regarded by them as attempts to force the "world" upon the country, producing havoc and chaos in their life. Their reaction to the modern school as the breeding ground of worldliness caused the construction of previously unknown parochial grade and high schools.

The Meidung trial of 1947, because it attracted universal attention, is described in greater detail on the following pages. It may serve as an example of Old Order Amish thought and behavior, and especially as a reaction to interference from without; furthermore, it shows how the surrounding culture, through the agency of the state, influences, affects, and molds Amish mores.

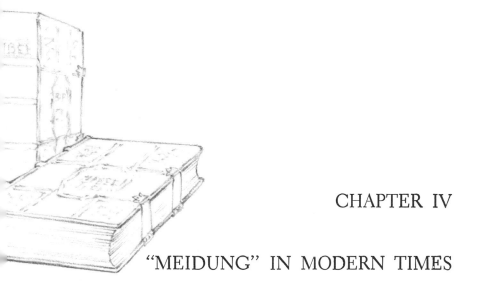

CHAPTER IV

"MEIDUNG" IN MODERN TIMES

Cause

A stirring incident involving Old Order Amish society and demonstrating the desire of the group to guard its customs within a narrowly confined rural setting was the celebrated "Meidung" case of 1947. The trial once again brought Amish life and religion to the scrutiny of the general public. On March 24, 1947, an Amish farmer, Andrew J. Yoder, thirty-two years of age, brought action in the Common Pleas Court of Wooster, county seat of Wayne County, Ohio, against Old Order Amish Bishop John W. Helmuth, two preachers, John J. Nisley and Isaac I. Miller, and Deacon Emmanuel D. Wengerd, asking $40,000 damages and a court injunction against a boycott which he alleged had been organized against him throughout the Amish church.

The circumstances surrounding the boycott were described by Yoder: One of his seven children had been afflicted with poliomyelitis at an early age in 1942, and it was necessary to bring her to Wooster frequently for treatments. Because the rules of the church forbade Andy to own and operate an automobile, the transportation problem of these weekly thirty-mile round trips had become a formidable one. The Yoders thought they needed a car to give the girl the necessary treatments and a chance for normal existence. They withdrew from the Helmuth Amish congregation and became affiliated with the "Conservative Amish" group in the Bunkerhill district of adjacent Holmes County which did not forbid the ownership of automobiles among its members. This action the Yoders took of their own free will in 1942. But the bishop, preachers, and deacon would not tolerate Yoder's withdrawal. Instead they invoked Article 17 of the Dortrecht Confession of Faith against him in spite of the fact that he had not been expelled but had peacefully withdrawn.

The "Meidung"—mite, avoidance, shunning, boycott— had been in effect for about five years in 1947. Yoder charged in court that the purpose of the "Meidung" was to compel him "to submit to church officials in the management of his trade, religious and business affairs, and it excluded him from all social and business relations with the members of said church by persuasion and intimidation." His own brother had been requested to boycott and avoid him and to have no dealings with him and had been told that his refusal to do so would place him, the brother, under the ban and make him also an object of the boycott. More than that, Yoder declared, the church authorities had approached his father to demand he remove him, Andy, from the farm which he had been operating under lease.

Yoder listed other injurious instances of the application of the "Meidung": at farm sales old friends would speak, but then actually shun his company; at one funeral he had been forced to eat under an apple tree while the others had dined in the house; at another a farm hand had requested Andy to eat at a separate table in a corner of the room; at various threshings he had been made to eat in the cellar. Worst of all, and here the boycott had showed its ugliest side, he had not been able to obtain help for his own harvesting operations, and the men he did get to help him were likewise banned from the church.

Andy J. Yoder summed up the reasons for leaving the Old Order Amish church in this way: (1) he had needed an automobile to afford transportation and to facilitate his farming operations; (2) he had needed transportation to Wooster, fifteen miles distant, so that his daughter, crippled with polio, might have treatments; (3) he had been opposed to the rule of his church which prohibited male members from wearing rubber suspenders; (4) he had been against the boycott rule; (5) he had believed that he, too, had a natural and indefeasible right to worship God according to the dictates of his own conscience. Yoder estimated that the damage to him in the injury of his own health and in isolation from society had amounted to some $40,000. He had also asked the court that the defendants be immediately enjoined from continuing the boycott.

The plaintiff claimed that he, Yoder, ordinarily calm and easygoing, had dared to file suit because he could find no other way out of the strict application of "Meidung," which really had come to mean slow death for him in his rural setting. Many conferences had been held, previous to filing suit, between him and Charles C. Jones, former Wooster judge and Yoder's attorney, and Bishop Helmuth and other members of his district. "We were trying to settle the matter in a peaceful way, as the Amish try to live, but the boycott, under church ruling, was 'for life' and everyone backed up the bishop," said Judge Jones.

The conflict had reached a climax after Bishop Helmuth and Deacon Wengerd visited Yoder's father, Joseph. What happened at this first meeting has not been made known. However the two church officials had returned two weeks later to see if the father had ousted his son from the farm. Andy happened to be at his father's home on this occasion. Upon hearing how the bishop and deacon had tried to induce the father to drive the son off the farm, Yoder

99

became so angry that he grabbed the bishop by the beard and led him out of the door. This event capped the series of annoyances which led to the civil suit.

A first reply to Yoder's court petition in the local newspaper by an unknown spokesman for the Helmuth congregation termed Yoder's accusations "one-sided and misrepresented." It asserted further that it had long been the practice of the church "to help get crippled children, as well as older people, to the doctor or hospital by automobile or ambulance." The retort denied that the boycott banned church members from exchanging work with the boycotted neighbor, and, it added, Yoder's medical bills and other expenses could have been paid "had he remained faithful to the church." But it did not elaborate on this latter statement.

The defendant Helmuth church officials would not, at first, file an official court answer; moreover, they refused to be represented by legal counsel. The reasons for this were again stated by an unidentified spokesman, who maintained that the very existence of the whole Old Order Amish church, not just of one individual Amish district, was at stake and had been made the subject of an unwarranted attack. The letter appeared in the *Wooster Daily Record* of April 22, 1947:

> The Amish Church does not pretend to be a perfect church as all of us make mistakes as well as everyone else. But as everyone knows every church has rules and regulations which must be followed if we expect to keep up the rules of our forefathers as we believe should be done. Our Christian forebears were drowned, hanged, burned alive, and tortured in most brutal manners, but they did not hire lawyers to defend themselves. They stood for the truth and the questions which they were asked they answered with the truth which they could do without the assistance of a lawyer. They depended upon the law and the rules that Christ gave them which reads: Matthew 10:17, "But

beware of men; for they will deliver you up to the Councils, and they will scourge you in their synagogue; 18, And ye shall be brought before Governors and Kings for My sake, for a testimony against them and the gentiles; 19, But when they deliver you up,—Take no thought what or how ye shall speak; For it shall be given you in that same hour, what ye shall speak; 20, For it is not ye that speak, but the Spirit of your Father which speaketh in you."

This we believe applies to any Christian people of today the same as it did at that time when this law was given. We believe the honest kind of lawyers are perfectly right in their place and we can not do without them. But in a case like the Yoder case where the lawyers are going to take over church matters, we have our Christian faith from our forefathers together with the Laws of Christ. All we need to answer in this case is the truth—no matter what it leads up to—even imprisonment or fine.

Our forefathers came to America for freedom of religion—which we have had up to this time and with the Constitution of the United States which now stands under law protecting freedom of religion, we shall be very thankful for, whenever our constitution to freedom of religion falls, our nation will also fall with it, according to the Bible.

The defendants subsequently indicated that they would file answer to Yoder's charges, and they were given permission by the court to have additional time to prepare this in accordance with the form required by the court.

At last, on May 3, 1947, the defendant Old Order Helmuth church officials filed a reply in the common pleas court, Case No. 35747, without presentation by legal counsel. The defendant bishop, preachers, and deacon fully admitted putting Andrew J. Yoder under the ban by citing Article 17 of the Confession of Dortrecht and that thereby

he was shunned and boycotted by all faithful Amish. They made haste to deny, however, some of the implications that Yoder had brought forth in his suit. In the introduction of this document the church leaders asserted that Yoder could not voluntarily leave the church without having the ban or boycott put on him. They said in part:

> Defendants believed him [Andrew J. Yoder] when he accepted the Confession of Faith and he knew when he accepted the rules of the church that if he would sometime do things against the church and against what he first agreed to do that he would be expelled and the ban put upon him. He was old enough to understand what the confession of faith means and that the church would never consent to have him leave the church. . . . In short, the church must put away from among herself him that is wicked whether it be in doctrine or in life.

The brief ends with this revealing appeal to freedom of religion:

> We are very sorry that anyone should try to keep us from worshipping God in the way that our people have worshipped since 1632 A.D. but if we are to be persecuted for our belief in God we must make ourselves strong by reading the Scriptures and doing only those things which our conscience will let us do.
>
> We hope Honorable Judge that you will do only what is right and just and we pray that God will lead you to give out justice to our congregation and people.

> JOHN W. HELMUTH
> JOHN J. NISLEY
> ISAAC I. MILLER
> EMMANUEL D. WENGERD

Upon receipt of this answer from the defendants, the clerk of the court set November 5, 1947, for hearing the suit. Religious and other concerned persons in the city, county, and surrounding communities took an immediate interest in the "Meidung" case. It aroused such attention chiefly because the defendants had made it plain that they would not resort to the help of a lawyer. Opinion was divided. To some the case seemed to involve the constitutionally guaranteed freedom of religion, while to others it appeared to involve only the mores of a closely knit economic and social group. Some voices loudly maintained that the "Meidung" simply expressed the negative commands of taboo, as practiced by a farming community isolated in the hills of the county and away from the concourse of the world. All were eager to see whether the Wooster court would embroil itself in a religious and sectarian controversy, involving the larger aspects of civil liberties, or limit the issue to the question of mores. The trial date became one of more than casual attention in Wayne County.

The Trial

On November 5, 1947, the Common Pleas courtroom and galleries were filled to capacity; one sensed immediately that this was not an ordinary small-town trial. Common Pleas Judge Walter J. Mougey, of Alsatian Mennonite descent himself, sat on the bench. The twelve jurors, nine men and three women, were all from outside of Wooster. The plaintiff, Andy Yoder, and his two attorneys, Charles C. Jones and George Barnard, occupied the places opposite the table around which the four defendants, Bishop John W. Helmuth, Preachers Isaac I. Miller and John J. Nisley, and Deacon Emmanuel D. Wengerd had taken their seats. They had no legal advisers. To the last it was doubted whether they would appear in court at all. No notes, no papers, no documents marked them as participants in this strife, but their broad-brimmed black hats lay on the table.

The Amish leaders passed among themselves a worn coverless Bible and a diminutive pocket edition of the Dor-

trecht Confession of Faith. They were not familiar with court procedure, and the judge reminded them frequently of their privilege to ask questions of Yoder's witnesses. Among the twelve witnesses were Yoder's wife, Sarah Mellot, Yoder's aged father, Joseph, and his elder brother, Dan. Frequent flashes of photographers' bulbs made the defendants cringe and hide their faces.

Of all the people in the large room—and the courtroom ıs filled with numbers of College of Wooster students d faculty, townspeople, farmers, Amish and Mennonites, ıd reporters from the leading press associations and from ıighboring cities—the defendants were the center of atten- ɔn and offered the most unusual and poignant spectacle. he rather small, stocky Bishop Helmuth had long dark ıir bobbed far below his ears, and his white bald pate was offset by the ruddy complexion of his face. His full, straggly beard fell to about the middle of his chest. His straight nose and sharp eyes were a distinct contrast to his unkempt hair and clothes. Helmuth's speech and manners, however, showed a man of power and influence, one accustomed to holding attention. The stout Preacher Miller had a rather jovial, happy, childlike appearance with his rotund features. The bangs stroked aside his forehead added to the round- ness of his appearance. But his high-pitched, weak voice was disappointing. More impressive was the Preacher Nisley, over six feet tall, with gaunt, pale, disturbed features. The unruly bristling hair and tousled beard gave him an almost prophetic appearance. It was he who attracted everyone's attention with his clear, full-throated voice, his stumbling at times over the English language, when the gestures of his unusually strong hands had to help him. The inner struggle he was experiencing showed itself in his troubled expres- sions. The tall Deacon Wengerd, with a graying beard and hair, offered a timid and delicate appearance. His voice was unusually thin, and he seemed unable to assert himself. From their general conduct one drew the conclusion that the men were average farmers, totally out of place in the courtroom to which their group practices had inadvertently brought them. One sensed, also, their assurance of having acted in the name of their faith and for the well-being of their own district.

The plaintiff, Andy Yoder, offered a marked contrast to the economically secure and socially accepted Amish leaders. He was a frail, small figure, pale and worried, but with a distinct and clear voice. The shorter cut of his hair and the trimming of his beard bespoke his membership in the less restrictive Conservative Amish Mennonite church. In his manner he showed signs of the ostracism which had made him feel like a "whipped dog." Even had he not spoken of the personal effects of the ban, his bearing would have revealed them. He seemed extremely young to be the father of seven children. His wife, Sarah, was a small woman, pleasant and cheerful looking. She wore the prescribed white prayer cap and was dressed in the plain purple colors characteristic of the Amish, but the buttons of her dress and jacket showed she had left the strict Old Order group where no buttons are tolerated on outer garments. Andy's father, bald and with a full white beard, represented the oldest group of Amish present.

The stage for the remainder of the trial was set by Attorney Jones who made the first charge:

> Andrew Yoder has lived ever since he was three years old on the Yoder Farm, which has been in the family for seventy-five years. He is thirty-three years old, is married and has seven children. Andy had a daughter Lizzie, who was a year old in 1942. Lizzie had to be brought to Wooster for medical treatment twice a week. Andy bought a 1937 Chevrolet car to do this— and was banned and shunned by his fellow church members, despite the fact that he had left his church and joined a more liberal one—(the Beachy Church)— in Holmes County. Article 17 of the Confession of Faith meant that the boycott or "Meidung" extended

to all congregations of the church. If Andy went to buy lumber for example, he couldn't get it; if he tried to get his or his family's shoes fixed, he could not get it done, and if anyone would help him, then that respective person was likewise put under the ban. Once when Andy pitched wheat the man on the wagon would first let it lie awhile, so that he could say he had not taken it from Andy. Hence the defendants have interfered with his means of making a living, his father was to chase him off the farm, and he could not get any help from his neighbors at harvest time; with his family life, his father and mother were ordered to have nothing to do with him, although living in a double house, and although the daughter needed constant attention, a brother boycotted him for more than five years; with his social life, at meal times he had to eat in the cellar, or after the meal, because his Amish neighbors were not allowed to eat or speak with him. The defendants have so upset his chances as guaranteed under the Constitution that they have even ruined his health, he has stomach ulcers.

The attorneys pointed out that this suit was not an action against any church—but it so happened that all the defendants were members of the Old Order Amish faith.

Bishop Helmuth's rebuttal address to the jury was brief: "I am sorry that this occasion is on hand. We feel that we will stand on Articles 16 [Excommunication from the Church] and 17 [Shunning] of the Confession of Faith written in Dortrecht, Holland, in 1632."

The four defendants were the first to take the witness chair. The questioning revolved mainly in establishing an affirmative answer on these two points: (1) Did the defendants put the ban on Andy Yoder and on others who would not boycott Andy? (2) Did the four defendants know at the time of placing the ban on the plaintiff that he had an invalid daughter whose plight necessitated his buying a car and having to withdraw from his original congregation? The testimony of defendants and other witnesses to these questions seemed incontrovertible and corroborated the original charge.

The defendants were reluctant to answer. Their most common remarks were, "We have nothing to say," or, "The Confession of Faith," or, "The Bible." They had to admit, however, that they had put the ban on Andy Yoder. They displayed an unshakable belief in the "Christian-ness" and righteousness of the "Meidung" practice of their church. They tried to justify their action by the fact that it was done for the good of Andy's soul. When Attorney Barnard objected, "What if Andy's soul had gone in this state to its Maker?" the audience was amused, but Bishop Helmuth refused to answer. Later, however, the Bishop interrupted with the remark: "We ought to obey God more than man." The four defendants pointed out that Andy's offense had been that he had joined the Old Order church in his youth and then later had left it. Preacher Nisley, in a breaking voice, climaxed the defendants' testimony: "I have lost sleep—I have thought over it—I have read the Scriptures—I have prayed to God for a way—and every time I wanted a way I would run up against a wall. Because when I was down on my knees—and I could say all this better in German—when we go down on our knees to be baptized, we don't go down for the fun of it."

It was clearly established that Andy's sin was in his departure from the Old Order Amish group. Only repentance and a return to the habits and customs of the original flock could atone for this. Amish friends of Andy who had refused to shun him and had therefore been excommunicated had been reinstated to full membership upon repentance and confession of their wrongdoings.

Flaws in the Old Order Amish system came pronouncedly into the open during the trial. Amish insistence on the righteousness of their own rules and the examples of their forefathers showed their greater emphasis on custom rather

107

than religion. Yet the origins and reasons for these behavior patterns were obscure and indefinite even to these men. None of the defendants could give any reason or explanation for the sinfulness of owning an automobile. Furthermore, none of the defendants was willing to comment on why the group would not grant salvation to a person, no matter how devout, who believed in the identical Confession of Faith and followed the same leaders, Menno Simons and Jakob Ammann, but were not of the same sectarian group. "All Andy Yoder needed to do was to live a Christian life and this controversy would all have vanished," was the most incriminating testimony the Preacher Nisley brought against the plaintiff. "Christian life," meant here, however, not a life of some particular merit or virtue, but simply the unquestioned adherence to the isolationist rural idiosyncrasies of the Old Order Amish. The objection by Attorney Barnard that Menno Simons himself had been a Catholic priest and by his change had given a precedent to Andy Yoder seemed to confuse the defendants; it had not occurred to these men that their forebears had not always been of the Anabaptist persuasion, nor had these men ever been asked to justify to an outsider their own mode of behavior, their moral code, or the mores of their rurally separated group.

Final arguments were offered on the afternoon of the second day. All four defendants took advantage of the privilege to address the jury in their own behalf. They expressed their regret that this case had come to court; all four of them were close to tears as they quoted the "Law of God" in support of shunning and excommunication as prescribed in their Confession of Faith. "We are God-fearing men," said Preacher Nisley, "and what I believe I can't change. If Andy Yoder's defiance of the church laws in the use of an automobile to carry an invalid daughter to a doctor had been a brother sin between Andy and me, we might have made it up. But when Andy went down on his knees and confessed in baptism all this [pointing to the Confession of

108

Faith] to be right, we had nothing else to do with it. The matter is between Andy and God—I am praying to God that the church and the jury do right. I am grateful that we have an order like this court. We also must have that kind of order in the church," concluded Preacher Nisley. Three of the four defendants uttered apocalyptic warnings of woe should freedom of religion vanish from the nation. Bishop Helmuth spoke last. He closed his brief statement with these words: "I have no hard feelings against Andy Yoder. I feel sorry for this affair and hope we can keep our religious freedom. I believe I lost more health and have been more worried than Andy Yoder has since he left the church. I wish the grace of God to you all."

The attorneys for the plaintiff in their limited arguments appealed to the jury: "You are called on to stop this most vicious practice of modern times—the 'Meidung' or shunning ban. This is psychological warfare; this is slavery; in the United States we abhor war, and we have long since abolished slavery." The audience became restless when one lawyer remarked: "Next to the Confession of Faith, written 315 years ago, the Amish worship the 'almighty dollar.'" Thereupon the bailiff quickly moved toward the gavel but found no occasion to exercise his authority. All listened intently to such pleading as: "They will start no more bans, if they have to pay enough to make them think."

The lateness of the hour prevented the presiding judge from charging the jury. At nine o'clock the following morning, the third day of the trial, the case was resumed. Plaintiff and defendants were in their customary seats. Every available space was occupied by spectators. In his charge to the jury Judge Mougey began: "The eyes of many people today are upon you and this court. They are waiting to see what will be done here. I therefore caution you to exercise the utmost care and discretion because your verdict in this case will have in the future a great deal to do with our form of government and what we may expect." The jurors were charged by the Judge with deciding whether or not the four

defendants (1) did conspire together and "by their acts did invade and violate the civil rights of the plaintiff and cause him injury and loss; (2) if such acts did cause him injury and loss, then you must determine what is the proper amount of damages due him."

As legal basis for the jury's deliberations, Judge Mougey cited the first article of the Bill of Rights of the federal Constitution—"Congress shall make no law respecting an establishment of religion, or prohibiting the free exercise thereof"—and Article I, Section 7 of the Ohio State Constitution (Ohio Code, Vol. 11, page 112)—"All men have a natural and indefeasible right to worship God according to the dictates of their own conscience. No person shall be compelled to attend, erect, or support any place of worship, or maintain any form of worship against his consent, nor shall any interference with the rights of conscience be permitted."

The judge particularly emphasized that

> no church may deny anyone any of these inalienable rights, including the right to withdraw if he chooses. When one interferes with the civil rights of another it is unlawful. . . . Evil acts, dangerous to the common good, even when performed by a religious group are unlawful. In olden times the sacrifice of human life was sanctioned by the church. But no intelligent person would justify that practice in the 20th century. Human slavery existed in this country less than a hundred years ago, and was assumed sanctioned by churchmen. But the right to human life and liberty prevents such practices. The law also protects these rights. Sincerity of religious belief is not legal excuse to deny anyone his guarantee of legal rights. Each individual is entitled to his own beliefs, but when he attempts to put such beliefs into practice and affects the civil right of others, then it becomes unlawful.

It is worthy of note that Judge Mougey in his charge gave an entirely new interpretation of the Mennonite Confession of Faith when he stated, "Nowhere in the Dortrecht Confession of Faith is it stated . . . that bishops, deacons, or preachers are given authority to enforce the regulations of the church. It appears to be addressed to the conscience of the individual." And he ruled further, "Under the right of freedom of religion, the plaintiff had a right to leave the Helmuth congregation, to buy a car, without being disciplined. He also had the right to unrestricted business and social intercourse."

Judge Mougey directed the jury to weigh the evidence carefully in the light of the law, telling them that their sole concern was the civil suit for $40,000 damages filed against the four defendants of the Helmuth district Old Order Amish Church. The injunction for the lifting of the "Meidung" or ban was the concern of the court, not the jury. "It is important that the defendants be fairly treated and not be made to pay excessive damages. Now, in the event that you find the plaintiff has failed to prove his case by the evidence, then in that case of course you will find for the defendants," said the judge, concluding his forty-five minute charge to the jury.

The jury within one hour and twenty-five minutes returned a unanimous verdict for the plaintiff, awarding him $5,000 damages. Judge Walter J. Mougey thanked them for the decision and commented: "I hope you have arrived at a correct verdict and, if I am any judge of the evidence, you have." In connection with the verdict the judge ordered the four churchmen to abandon their boycott against Andy Yoder and granted an injunction restraining them from imposing any boycott against Andy Yoder which would deny him the right to religious liberty or deprive him of any business or social relations with his fellow church members. He also ordered the church officials to withdraw any order instructing their congregation to boycott Yoder for alleged violation of church rules. "The court believes that this mat-

ter of religious freedom is an individual matter," Judge Mougey concluded.

Andy Yoder's comment when interviewed after the successful conclusion of his suit was, "I am satisfied. I believe the injunction will do more good than the damages. I think they [the churchmen] will think some time before they put on any more bans." When asked if he thought the church officials would obey the injunction, Yoder replied, "If they don't they are awful narrow-minded." Numerous Amish, some of them under the ban themselves, and many other Mennonites were in the crowded court room. One of them was heard to say: "This will mean a revolution in our church throughout the world." It was even rumored that some of those under the ban were awaiting the outcome of the trial before proceeding with similar court action.

During the reading of the verdict none of the defendants was present. They had obtained permission to be absent from the conclusion of this trial caused by the possession of an automobile and to which they had heretofore driven in a rented car.

The journal entry, signed by Judge Mougey and attorneys Charles C. Jones and George Barnard reads as follows:

> The Second Cause of Action herein came on for hearing before the Court and on consideration of same, and the evidence submitted, the Court finds for the Plaintiff on this Cause of Action, and that the injunction prayed for should be granted. It is, therefore, ordered, decreed, and adjudged, that the Defendants, and each of them, are hereby permanently restrained and rejoined from further entering into a conspiracy or common plan or purpose of "shun," "mite," "avoid," or boycott the Plaintiff, and/or to so join with any others in doing so and/or to order and direct any member of the Amish Faith to so "shun," "mite," "avoid," or boycott the said Plaintiff, and/or to threaten any of the said members of the Amish Faith that if they do

112

not do as ordered or directed by placing the "shun," "mite," "avoidance" or boycott on said Plaintiff that said member or members themselves respectively will be subject to the "shun," "mite," "avoidance" or boycott.

A mandatory injunction is also allowed and decreed ordering said Defendants to revoke and annul any and all orders or directions that they, or each of them, have given to any member or members of the Amish Faith to "shun," "mite," "avoid," or boycott the said Plaintiff and further to inform said members so ordered or directed of said revocation and annulment. To all of which ruling the Defendants except.

Epilogue

The Amish "Meidung" case was not actually settled in court. Its true conclusion came months later. Andrew Yoder had won a verdict from the Amish leaders awarding him $5,000 in damages. These stalwart leaders had always contended that the affair was God's doing, and, since the worldly powers had interfered and decided the matter, they themselves would do nothing further about it. The verdict was not appealed, but neither were steps taken to comply with the court order.

Accordingly toward the end of December, 1947, Sheriff Wayne Warner of Holmes County was ordered to execute a sale of the chattel property of Bishop John Helmuth. The farm and land on which Helmuth lived were not included in the court action because the land was under mortgage. After appraisals by Robert Read and Walter R. Finley, and the customary ten-day publication, a great crowd of people, buyers, curious spectators, and newspaper men alike, gathered on the premises of the Helmuth farm, located just south of Mt. Eaton, Wayne County, but in Holmes County. The bishop had left the scene early in the morning, but

his wife and daughter had remained to witness the tragic sale which would impoverish them.

The sheriff's report of the sale shows the exact items sold, including 226 items with 31 sums of money received. The larger amounts of the rather poor sale showed that eight hogs brought $550, 130 shocks of corn $91, the bishop's surrey brought $36 after spirited bidding by two graybeards, one of whom was related to the bishop; another buggy sold for $41, two Holstein cows for $150, one Jersey cow for $85, three horses for a total of $100, a mower for $35, 51 shocks of fodder for $51, a corn sheller for $12.50, a buckboard wagon for $5, bantam chickens for 35 cents a piece. Many of the essentials of farm life, a milk cow and a work horse, a hand plow and the indispensable horse and buggy were bought back by Helmuth's wife's brother. The total amount raised was $2,359.61, which, after the deduction of costs of $83.10, left a total of $2,276.51 to be credited on the $5,000 judgment.

A month later, January 23, 1948, the sheriff's department of Wayne County started listing the chattel property of Preacher John J. Nisley, the second of the defendants. The sale could after the customary ten days take place for appraisal and advertising. If Nisley's chattels would have fallen short of meeting the remaining amount to pay the full $5,000 judgment, the law would then have had to wait five weeks to advertise the real property which had been appraised at $8,000. Preacher Nisley owned his large and prosperous farm outright, and hence it was subject to court indemnity.

But suddenly there came surprising dramatic action. On January 29, 1948, Preacher Nisley appeared in Sheriff Edwin Mills' office with $2,939.04 in cash, the exact amount needed to complete the claim. He made no comment on how he had secured the money or why he had taken steps to comply with the judgment. His funds included $2,885.98 remaining on the judgment plus interest, $10 for appraisers, eighty cents for appraisers' oaths, $2.88 for mileage for levying, and $28.86 in "poundage," the term applied to the 1 per cent which goes to the sheriff's department according to statute for handling such transactions. Officially no one knows who paid the money, but it is reported that a prominent businessman who had extensive dealings with the Amish paid the remainder.

Preacher Nisley's capitulation to modern law in paying this share of the judgment came a little more than a week after four Amish churchmen from Lancaster County, Pennsylvania, had visited in Wayne County. They had come to Wooster on January 17 and 18 to examine the court records and on a second trip they held conferences with various Amish leaders and with Bishop Helmuth and Andy Yoder. To the amusement of a few observers these men from Lancaster County, Pennsylvania, had twice come in a big rented motor vehicle although possession of an automobile is as sinful for them as it is for the Ohio Amish. Thus closed the official court action in which modern American civil law had declared lagging, damaging rural customs harmful to an individual's freedom and happiness.

However, although Andy Yoder, the plaintiff, had won out over his persecutors, personal tragedy stalked his family. The small girl whose illness precipitated the quarrel died at the home of her parents after a brief illness, April 5, 1949. She was then seven years old. Since her birth she had been afflicted with a malformation of the hip bone (the original diagnosis of polio seems to have been incorrect), and it was when her father purchased an automobile to transport his daughter to a doctor in Wooster that he came into conflict with the rules of the church. The Amish "Meidung" case, the public dispute between Amish mores and American civil law, was the direct outcome.

It is hard for an observer to judge whether the payment of the money compensated Yoder for his physical and emotional injuries at the hands of the leaders of the Amish district. The loss of his child only added to his personal tragedy.

115

During the same summer of 1949 Preacher Nisley lost his wife through death, an added sorrow for the man to whom this trial was the greatest spiritual ordeal of his life. He himself soon followed his wife, and Bishop Helmuth died the following year.

As in the earliest Amish history, when Jakob Ammann insisted on the strictest observance of "Meidung" in 1693, so in 1947 more seemed to be at stake than can be read from the court records. The outsider cannot know how much personal animosity between Bishop Helmuth and Andy Yoder and the rest of the Amish community was involved. Bishop Helmuth had moved into his district in Holmes County as a farmer of only 55 mortgaged acres, with a small family but strong convictions concerning his group's mores. The fight over the "Meidung" reached the court only after the real leader of the Amish community, Preacher Eli J. Miller (mentioned in chapter iii), had died. Apparently there exists, too, a rivalry between Wayne and Holmes County Amish, with Bishop Helmuth living in Holmes and Andy Yoder living in Wayne County. It was also said that Bishop Helmuth expected the Amish to come to his rescue to prevent the sheriff's sale, which seemed to him to disgrace the whole Amish world. For unknown reasons this help did not come until after the sale, when the greater part of the aid came from his wife's brothers. On the other hand life for the plaintiff, Andy Yoder, is still isolated. Old Order Amish avoid him, but the new group of "Conservative Amish" to which he belongs is growing stronger.

CHAPTER V

COMMUNITY LIFE AND ORGANIZATION

Sunday Observance

One discovers the cohesiveness of the Old Order Amish peasant society best in the fortnightly district meeting. This assembly is a continual source of Amish strength and unity, the chief refuge from worldly encroachment. It is unthinkable for any Amish man or woman to stay away from the lengthy Sunday gathering.

Sunday observance in Amishland is more than compliance with the Third Commandment. Without this regular assembly of all members of the Gemei, Amish society would soon disintegrate. For social as well as religious reasons, attendance must be complete. But Sunday observance is also the scrupulous following of the commandment for the Sabbath: "Six days shalt thou labor, and do all thy work, but the seventh is the sabbath of the Lord thy God; in it thou shalt not do any work." Accordingly, the Amish perform only the most unavoidable chores on Sunday, such as feeding the livestock and milking the cows. Many do not send milk to the creamery even when they belong to a dairy co-operative or to some other regular milk route. Similarly, neither threats of thunderstorms in harvest time nor extra field work made necessary by the use of slow, horse-drawn equipment prevails against the traditional Sabbath customs or keeps a member away from the Gemei. On Sunday also the Amish seldom travel very far from home; the Amish-owned bus line does not operate at all on the Sabbath. Although milk may be heated and coffee made on the day itself, other cooked food for Sunday is prepared the day before. The Amish hesitate even to call a doctor or veterinarian on Sunday.

Between Labor Day and Easter the Old Order Amish districts hold their meetings in the homes of the members. During the warmer months of the year, they gather in one or another of the large bank barns. The rounds are arranged so that each family of the Gemei entertains in either house or barn once a year. The host family also provides dinner for the assemblage.

When a district grows too large for convenient accommodation or when some of the members locate too far away from the original district area, the Amish give serious thought to splitting the district and founding a new one. Such divisions account for the organization of the east-central Ohio Amish into forty-two districts. The divisions so made are matters of convenience and do not entail hard feelings or animosities. Dividing lines are drawn along country roads or highways, creeks or ranges of hills, but the outer boundaries of the new district are left open. The older districts, toward the center of Amishland, are firmly established within certain spatial limits on all sides.

The Old Order Amish, or House Amish, as they are also called, do not have church buildings. During the two centuries of suppression and persecution in Europe, the Anabaptists had to hold their meetings under the shade of darkness. Calling attention to themselves by means of special modes or styles of dress, conveyances, or by the use of formal meeting houses was out of the question. Moreover, houses of worship were forbidden to them by law even after they were assured of life and limb. At the same time, the originators of Anabaptism in Switzerland had themselves agitated against all outer forms of ritual and ceremony in the exercise of the Christian faith. With the abolition of the other externalities which had accumulated in the medieval church building, it was only one further, logical step to abandon the meeting house itself.

Yet it is interesting that one of the first Amish congregations on the Ohio scene did what it could not do in the Old World: it constructed a meeting house in 1816 in Green Township, Wayne County. The first members of this congregation had arrived in Ohio only a short time before, in 1812. Since then the Oak Grove congregation has advanced with the times and has had a phenomenal impact upon modern America, as well as upon the whole Mennonite world (see chap. i). Another Mennonite group which contrasts with the Old Order Amish on this point and yet is close to them in other ways is the sect of "Conservative Amish." Known also as "Church Amish," the group is increasing in membership. The bearded men and hooded women who compose its number are permitted to drive to service in automobiles.

The Amish rearrange the downstairs of their homes to accommodate a whole congregation, but they do not arrange their homes or barns to simulate other Protestant churches. They know nothing of altars with crosses, candelabra, flowers, or draperies; neither do they have elevated platforms, pulpits, or lecterns. The deacon holds his Bible himself, and the preachers are unhampered by notes or manuscripts in their sermons. The Amish do not use bells, organs, or pianos, and incense, holy water, special garments, and other vestiges of ceremonial are missing.

The Amish do not expect that each member family can provide seats for all members. The Gemei owns a set of plain wooden benches available for gatherings on Sunday and for weddings and funerals. These they use as needed, transporting them on a farm wagon; during the intervening time they store the benches in a barn.

For the Sunday service the host places the benches in long rows in the cleared middle section or threshing den of the upper story of the barn. The worshipers do not sit by families but by age groups, separated by sex; men and women face each other. The father will take care of his young sons; the mother, of the infants and small girls. The leaders of the service and the visiting preachers sit around a table at the far end. The seats are hard, of course, and the setting is plain, but both qualities are familiar to the austere and hardy Amish. Still the barn doors on either side permit sufficient ventilation and a cooling breeze. A bucket of drinking water and a dipper are placed by the entrance to refresh the thirsty.

The meeting itself is characterized by its utter simplicity. No musical interludes, except hymn singing, distract the service. No collections are made. One senses the likeness of the Amish meeting to the practices of the early Christians when they gathered to worship as these are reported in the opening chapters of the Acts of the Apostles. On the other hand, the Amish service, with its barnyard setting and its great length, is as different from modern Protestant rites as are the people themselves from modern, city-bred Americans. The two sermons and the long scriptural reading that divides them consume too much time according to twentieth-century standards. The monovoiced singing of sixteenth century hymns before and after the preaching is dreary and painful to modern ears.

That the modern age does somewhat influence the service is indicated in a recent Amish publication. *Handbuch für Prediger* ("Preacher's Manual," 1950) attempts to bring some order into Amish church life. It lists possible scriptural texts and hymns for any given Sunday. The Manual also advises that the total preaching time be no more than three hours at biennial meetings and even less at fortnightly gatherings. It even berates ministers for exceeding seventy-five minutes if they have not planned their sermons thoroughly or have given scant attention to content or manner of delivery. Preachers often hide, the Manual asserts, in the New Testament words: "Do not be anxious how you are to speak or what you say; for what you are to say will be given to you in that hour; for it is not you who speak, but the spirit of your father speaking through you." The Amish have always laid this passage at the very basis of their life, education, and selection of leaders; the Manual, one gathers, interprets this quotation in an entirely different manner and presumes an authoritarian interpretation wholly foreign to Amish thinking.[1]

The sermons by the leaders keep alive and nourish the consciousness of the Amish way of life. The virtues and values of membership in the Old Order Gemei are intensively brought to the awareness of all members of the group. The preachers emphasize that for the Amish the modes of labor and religion are one, implying seclusion from the concourse of the world, a life of toil and hard personal labor, frugality and simplicity. The Bible, in the example of Sodom and Gomorrah, condemns to eternal damnation ambitions that lead to the sins of cities and the world. Because they believe that yielding to one temptation will lead to another and finally to a complete abandonment of all wholesome virtues, the Amish are exhorted to resist innovations created and disseminated by the city. A farm in a hilly country setting and its attendant labor are the surest safeguards against the evil outer world. Unity and uniformity are maintained so well partly because attendance at these sermons is nearly perfect. To absent one's self would indicate devious behavior. Bound together by ties of tradition and sentiment, each member of the district finds himself intimately linked with and supported by conservative neighbors.

The ministers never tire of plumbing the writings of Old and New Testaments and those of their own ancestors for

123

verifications of these preachings, and the congregations never seem to grow weary of hearing them. Nevertheless, the religious basis of Amish preaching is limited and eclectic. The Bible is, indeed, the true and inspired word of God, to be accepted as it stands in Luther's translation, not a tittle to be taken away. The Book of Genesis explains creation and man's place in it. The seven articles of Schleitheim and the eighteen articles of the Dortrecht Confession of Faith summarize the essential points of salvation. Like these, the rest of the Scriptures is found to give sanction to Amish views and customs. Should he emulate the lives of Jesus and the Apostles, heed the beatitudes of the Sermon on the Mount, and follow current Amish mores, heaven cannot be denied to the faithful man or woman. The Amish feel they come nearest to security and favor in the eyes of God and their Gemei when they adhere unswervingly to their presently approved traditions, achieve independence by owning their farms, and avoid idleness.

Twice a year, in springtime around Easter and in fall, each Amish district holds a plenary session. This is a longer and more intensive Sunday service than the biweekly meeting. It is preceded by a special day of fasting and meditation. All who have deviated from the true and narrow ways of Amish traditions and behavior find purification and sanctification on this occasion. Members who have personal disagreements affecting the well-being and good name of the group make their peace at this gathering, which is closed to outsiders. The plenary session is most important in the life and perpetuation of these people. Harmony and peace are vouchsafed in acts of footwashing and the love feast. With only the faithful participating, the celebration of the Lord's Supper is the symbolic attainment of oneness of Old Order Amish religion and life.

Whether at a plenary session or a biweekly meeting, it is remarkable with what interest the Amish follow a preacher's interpretation of Scripture, continuing to discuss it after the service is completed. The Amish are nevertheless

124

not totally immune to human boredom. One sometimes hears, after a lengthy discourse: "It was good, but it would have been better if it had been shorter." Although the Manual suggests twenty to thirty minutes for the preliminary sermon and one hour for the main sermon, there seems to be no instance of the first or "warm-up" sermon ever being that brief or of the second or "main" sermon being less than seventy minutes. In some meeting places a clock is now hidden in a convenient spot for the preachers to gauge the length of their remarks. Outsiders must wonder how men who have worked all week in field or barn, as have all their brethren, can stand in front of the Gemei and talk from fifty to seventy minutes on some scriptural topic.

The testimonials following the main sermon on Sunday morning constitute another important feature of Amish religious life. Only adult males and visiting ministers who feel inspired may speak, and the time is restricted by the lateness of the hour. The remarks often bring forward points of view and opinions about the biblical text which may have been overlooked by the day's preachers and which the member has found verified in his experience. When the group chooses new leaders, possible candidates and their qualifications are known through these exercises.

The communal meal following the conclusion of the formal religious service is indispensable in Old Order Amish rural life. Men and women sit on opposite sides of the table, but conversation across the table is practically non-existent; in some districts each group eats by itself. The tables consist of two benches moved together and covered with a white tablecloth. In former years the menu was surprisingly simple: large bowls of bread and milk, with accompanying relishes. Now varieties of cold cuts, ham, cheese, jellies, and bread, with a reminder of the sweets and sours of the Pennsylvania Dutch neighbors in the form of pickles, beets, carrots, celery, hard-boiled eggs, and greens, form the menu. Gourmet dishes find no place at this Sunday repast.

Because a large congregation must be served in shifts,

there is a convenient chance for the varying age groups to eat by themselves. This socializing continues throughout the day until the older members of each family turn their buggies homeward. Afterward the young folks stay for general merrymaking, without any exact curfew being imposed on them. If there are chores to be done at home, a dashing horse and a helpful friend may easily lighten the burden.

As indicated before, the Old Order Amish Gemei meets officially only every other Sunday. The free Sunday serves another vital feature of Amish life: visiting and keeping "Verwandtschaft und Freundschaft," relationship and friendship, alive. This is more than mere diversion and relaxation. Worshiping and visiting with members of districts far and wide in the Amishland are essential to the solidarity of the sect as a united, purposeful body. The men have opportunities to exchange information about farms, crops, weather; under discussion, too, are the weighty problems of public education, governmental regulations, highway safety, perhaps even national and international affairs, and topics which relate to the health and welfare of the whole Amish society. The women find a break in the monotony of rural isolation with ready homespun topics of children, family, gardens, and gossip. Young people have a chance to become acquainted, to play, perhaps to cast an eye about for a future mate. Vital or trivial news travels by buggy in the span of two weeks to the most remote member within the extensive east-central region of the Ohio Amishland.

To sit among the bearded, vigorous men and the hooded, gentle-appearing women during their Christian worship service, in barn or house, and to share their meal at a communal table, gives one an opportunity to understand the purpose and direction of these Christian primitivists. Here the visitor meets first-hand the strength embodied in the Protestant Reformation and the special stability of the Old Order Amish which seems to manifest the truth of the Apostle's exhortation: "Food and covering and being therewith content" (I Timothy 6:8). Extreme simplicity and

126

uniformity of appearance and behavior seem to convey inner strength and fortitude.

When the individual Amish man or woman leaves the company of his neighbors, he feels reaffirmed in the claims of his life and faith. The man who sat next to him during the preaching service, to whom he passed the bread and with whom he exchanged opinions and information he sees again on Monday performing the same chores across the fence that engage his own energy. He does not want to excel him but only to put before him the model of a good farmer. As long as he has these opportunities—to work the soil and make a livelihood, to meet again in the Gemei, to eat and to visit with his neighbor—so long is he untroubled and assured of the rightness of his way of life.

MINISTERS AND RULERS

The Old Order Amish Gemei or district, as was seen in the preceding section, is an unaffiliated, self-sufficient, self-governing unit. At the same time it may be mentioned that the Gemei as such possesses no property and has no funded wealth or indebtedness. It collects no tithes or pledges of support. It maintains no local or national programs or institutions. Its ministers do not receive remuneration for their preaching. The individual district, thus, has no financial outlays and obligations. It is true that individual families contribute labor or money in cases of emergency, but only voluntarily.

The Gemei preserves its autonomy through the pattern of local organization which it has inherited from the past and to which it clings today with unshakable tenacity. The overseers of this narrowly defined group come from its own membership; there are no intruders from the outside. Instead the Gemei itself chooses its own guides and rulers from among those bred in the ways of the district.

Customarily there are four recognized leaders: the "Armen Diener, Diakon"—servant of the poor—deacon; the

127

two "Diener zum Buch"—servants of the book—preachers; and the "Völlige Diener, der Bischof"—complete servant—the bishop. The three functions of leadership are, correspondingly, "Der Armen Dienst," or "Der Dienst zu den Armen"—the service to the poor; "Der Dienst zum Buch" —service to the book, i.e., the Bible; and "Der Völlige Dienst und zum Buch," or "Das Bischofamt"—the bishop's office and service to the book.[2] The highest office, as the name implies, is the "Völlige Diener," the complete servant, or minister with full powers. These "Diener," or "servants," do indeed serve their communities. Guardians and ministers of the community welfare, they represent leadership both in the Amish way of life and in farming enterprises.

The bishop is ordained in the name of the Lord and the Gemei. He alone baptizes, marries, and buries members of the group; he alone can expel those who do not fit into the strict sectarian pattern or receive back into the flock those sinners and apostates who have repented. He has, thus, ultimate power over all matters pertaining to Amish life. His word is law, implying salvation or damnation. His prescriptions concerning appearance, manners, and behavior, or machinery, tools, and implements must be followed. It is he who controls the form, style, shape, and color of costumes and garments.

The bishop is much aware that the Divine will and appointment rest on him, showing this in the dignity and authority with which he conducts his office. By God's will he has the "keys of the kingdom, what you bind shall be bound in heaven, and what you lose shall be lost in heaven." In consequence, both in earthly and spiritual matters, by personal conduct and in his farming venture, he tries to be a model of godliness and a living proof that the Amish way of life is right, pleasing to God, and exemplary. It can be clearly observed, too, that the greater the bishop's success in temporal affairs so much the more effective is his influence as spiritual leader.

The two preachers—"Diener zum Buch"—have the office of interpreting the Bible to the congregation in its fortnightly meeting, to lead in prayer, to speak to the faithful members through the mouth of the forefathers—"durch die Altväter zu reden"—to distribute the wine at the biennial plenary session, to visit the sick, widows, and orphans, and to assist with the marriage and burial of members.[3]

The office of the deacon—"Diener zu den Armen"—is also closely defined. The deacon has over-all responsibility for widows and orphans and collects alms. He looks after the temporal welfare of any member who experiences special hardship through illness, fire, or other mishap. Upon destruction of a barn by lightning, for example, he will solicit material aid from the congregation and manual help from neighboring districts. Or, if a member becomes negligent in farming practices, should he permit his fences and buildings to deteriorate, the deacon will admonish him and try to assist him to preserve the good name of the Amish community.

The deacon is also charged to settle grievances and to pacify quarrels within the Gemei. It is he who assists young brothers and sisters in the faith when they are about to be married and their banns have been announced in the congregational meeting, and it is he who pours the water through the cupped hands of the bishop at a baptism. At the biennial communion service, he provides the bread and wine.[4] Though he does read the Scriptures during the Sunday service, the deacon does not preach, unlike the other three officials. On the other hand, he is charged with watching that in doctrine and sermons the Lord's word is correctly interpreted and not falsified.

These four leaders of the Gemei consult together before or after every fortnightly congregational assembly. In seclusion upstairs in the farmhouse, they ponder the affairs of the district while the Gemei engages in singing hymns below in the house or in the barn. The appearance of the leaders marks the beginning of the preaching service.

129

The bishop and the preachers stand before the congregation and expound the Bible for from forty to seventy minutes every other Sunday. Actually free to choose their own texts and topics, the preachers find some guidance in tradition and the Manual. Another guide to the use of texts for preaching, as well as for the choice of hymns for various Sundays, is found in *Der Neue Amerikanische Calender*, a pamphlet edited by the Old Order Amishman J. A. Raber of Baltic, Ohio, and found in practically every Amish home.

For the preachers, the most important items in the Bible, those most frequently expounded and interpreted, are the Our Father (Matthew 5), the Prayer of the High Priest (John 17), the Conversion of Paul (Acts 9), the Prodigal Son (Luke 15), and How To Overcome Enemies (Luke 22:41). Apart from these texts it is important for them to know the events of early Jewish history, for the Amish like to compare themselves with the persecuted Jews of the Exodus on the way to a better land.

Believing in the inspiration and binding power of the Bible, yet confining their attention only to certain appropriate and well-worn biblical passages, the Old Order Amish preachers are not apt to lead their people away from their biblically sanctioned mores into modern practices. Moreover, the preachers will not turn to previously unexplicated biblical passages to find new interpretations or commands for life. Literalism in the interpretation of a few selected passages and strict adherence to the ways of the fathers in the "Ordnung" or "Gebrauch"—order or custom—are their watchwords.

These leaders of the Old Order Amish are not trained to be critical in evaluating their concepts of God or the universe or of man's relation to them. Their theology, in so far as an individual leader may have conceived a system of religion, is that which was long ago developed by the early Anabaptist reformers and which is set out in the seven points of the Schleitheim Confession of 1527 and in the more elaborate eighteen articles of the Dortrecht Confession of 1632. In Amish eyes, to these sources of faith nothing needs to be added or may be subtracted. The present-day Amish leaders, as well as their parishioners, accept unquestioningly the traditional doctrines. Moreover, with the accomplishment of the Reformation, they feel, the path to salvation was laid out; and, again from the point of view of the Amish, that path is the Amish way of life. Thus, doctrine and the existing patterns of the sect's life are considered indivisible; acceptance of ancient beliefs and conformity to current life patterns are the hallmarks of the highest personal perfection. Amish preaching, directed toward this attainment, is marked with a statism or legalism not unlike that of Old Testament Judaism: salvation is assured by strict adherence to the externalities of current behavior approved by the group. These forms have become identified with—and indistinguishable from—the essentials of Amish faith and salvation. The function of the leaders is to preserve this formalism, and their duty is well served by the insistence on, and strict advocacy of, a restricted literalism.

The Amish congregation chooses its leaders in two stages. A nominating vote is followed by a drawing of lots by the nominees. All baptized male members are eligible for election. Thus the district makes its preferences known first, but the choice is made by the Lord. Authority once being granted, there is no recourse from a disapproved or ineffectual leader. Vacancies occur only by the death of an incumbent, or through serious physical disability, the natural splitting of a district as a result of growth, or a leader's moving to another location.

In selecting possible servants, the members of a congregation are admonished to look to men who are "healthy in their faith" and who have managed and arranged their homes and affairs well. The Manual for Preachers stipulates no other qualification for these high offices. Not only may any baptized male become a minister, but, upon joining the group at baptism, each young man must promise to accept office if the lot should fall to him. Similarly each

131

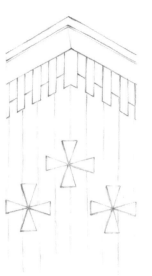

young woman member promises to bear with whoever shall be elected as a leader. Thus, a preacher is never called from another congregation, and previous experience, education, or training are of no consideration. On the other hand, his brothers may ask about a possible candidate, "How much land does he own?" "Is he respected in the community for honest work and dealings?" "Do his children behave as Amish children should?" "Have he and his family strictly followed Amish ways?" or, "If the lot falls to this man, will he be a good representative of the district?" Such are the considerations which precede a voting.

Needless to say, the position of leader is of great prestige in the community. No greater claim to respectability can be made than to be able to name bishops and ministers among one's ancestors or immediate family. Both worldly approbation and assurance of orthodoxy are associated with these offices.

The election procedure is simple. At the appointed communion meeting all men and women are asked for their choice of candidate. The men who receive two or three votes are then led into a room in which there are as many Bibles as candidates. One of the Bibles contains a slip of paper with the prayer, "Lord, knower of all hearts, show whom thou hast chosen among these brethren, that one may receive this service to [the book, the poor, the bishop's office]."[5] The paper is placed near chapter 1, verse 26 of the Acts of the Apostles, which tells how the Apostles, after the death of Judas, filled the vacancy from a choice of two candidates: "And they cast lots for them, and the lot fell upon Matthias; and he was enrolled with the eleven apostles." Whoever draws the marked Bible is the new "Diener."

The simple ordination ceremony, which consists in the laying on of hands, is always presided over by a bishop and is carried out very simply. It may take place upon the visit by some bishop or on the return of the elected member to a former home and congregation. Preachers and deacons stand while they are ordained; the new bishop must kneel. A charge enumerating the duties of office is always pronounced, and hands are laid on "in the name of the Lord and of the Gemei."

There are both strengths and weaknesses in such a system of choosing a Diener. First of all, there need never be a lack of leaders. Amish groups, even as they settled along the frontier, never had to wait for a "mother church" to set up a parochial organization for them. If they did not actually emigrate under the leadership of a preacher, the families in a new locale soon elected one, waiting perhaps only until several families had arrived. A stronger point in favor of the selection of leaders and preachers from among the district's own male membership is that the individual members, as well as the district as a body, need not fear the guidance and rule of an unsympathetic outsider who lacks understanding of the ways of the district. One interesting result of this Amish insistence on local leadership is the differences between the Amish of Ohio and those of Pennsylvania, Indiana, and Iowa; but, whatever the differences, one can be sure that they are home-grown, that they have originated in the local setting, and that they have not been forced upon the group.

A weakness of the Amish system is the fact that it provides no opportunity for its leadership to assume responsibilities wider than those of the local district. But, from the Amish point of view, this limitation is a source of strength. Leadership is not drained off. The congregation remains one united body. During the course of the week the leaders, no matter how gifted, cannot be distinguished from other Amishmen. They wear no special garb or insignia; they are not addressed with special titles. They receive no material rewards for their spiritual labors. They tend their fields and barns and make their livings as farmers. On Sunday, however, these men stand before their fellows to expound the Scriptures and their religion as the guidance of

133

the holy Spirit and the experience gained in the daily chores move them to do.

Sometimes the method of choosing a Diener brings forward a real spiritual leader in the group. There have been Amish speakers who in elocution, wisdom, and biblical knowledge were of a very high quality. Moreover the office itself is of such importance that the new servant gives careful meditation and thought to his responsibilities. Believing in the inspiration of the holy Spirit who made the simple fisherman, Peter, go forth in strength and courage, he calls forth the best in himself. But the "casting of the lot" is apparently not always inspired. Men sometimes are selected who are neither capable of preaching nor inclined to do so, while others devout and gifted in mind and speech are passed over. There is no doubt, too, that in some instances elections have been influenced by the desire of younger men, sometimes composing a majority, to have relatively lenient leaders. The younger men may elect or try to elect one of their own number.

Splits caused by unalleged differences of opinion or interpretation occur as a result of just this sort of clash between liberal and conservative elements within a group. This splitting has resulted in the many Amish congregations which differ only in the degree and extent to which they stress conformity in externals. And it is natural that such diversity should arise where an uneducated clergy, untutored in biblical languages and historical scholarship, goes directly to the Bible for its guidance in all matters. The kaleidoscopic mixture of Wayne County Amish and Mennonites bears witness to this historic process.

The most consistent and the easiest approach for such untrained, rural overlords is to adhere rigidly to the status quo, or "Gebrauch," as they call it, the currently approved manners and morals, and to guard against all changes or innovations. Thus no detail of life on the farm is too slight to escape the watchful eye of the Amish leaders. The most insignificant or trivial item—a straight pin, a button, the flap of a pocket, a curl in the hair, a tiny glass window in the rear or side curtain of the buggy, a reflector on the rig, a clasp on the horse's harness, the pocket on a man's shirt, the band on the black hat, the trimming of the ragged beard—becomes meaningful. Conformity to the bishop's prescription about such things becomes a behavior essential to salvation. It is easy to see why the leaders exert such tremendous influence in the narrowly confined rural districts when their judgment on conformity or deviation is held to distinguish saint from sinner. It is easy also to see the basis of discontents.

But so long as the severe district unity we have described is maintained, the Old Order Amish will survive in America. Faith and customs will pass from father to son, from mother to daughter. A few tough-minded rebels may push beyond the barriers to more liberal ways, but most children will heed their elders and thus perpetuate the naïve, classically simple patterns of Amish rural life.

The Hymns of the "Ausbund"

A distinctive portion of the Amish Sunday meeting and one markedly different from its counterpart in the modern American Protestant service is the singing of hymns. These, sung in the Sunday district gatherings, at weddings and funerals, reveal once again deep roots in past tradition. Singing begins each meeting, and an hour does not always suffice for it; a final devotional act in song always terminates the religious service. An outsider finds it quite impossible to participate, no matter how trained vocally he may be or how much he would like to share in the experience. For one thing, the Amish abhor written notes. Moreover, the singing is strange and difficult, even to their own congregations, and virtually incredible to those outside their group. It is medieval in tone and rhythm, as out of touch with today's world as Amish dress and customs. Yet no one attempts to alter text or melody.

The hymnbook used exclusively by the Old Order Amish is known by the one German word, "Ausbund." The earliest complete, dated edition seems to be that of 1583.[6] One part of it, a group of some fifty-three hymns, however, was printed as early as 1564. The total number of songs in the Ausbund is 140, with an Appendix of six ballads added in the seventeenth century. This anthology of sectarian songs was printed in Europe until the nineteenth century. The first American edition was brought out by Christopher Sauer in Germantown, Pennsylvania, in 1742. Because of its small, thick format it is also known as "Das Dicke Buch" —the thick book, in contrast with "Das Dünne Büchlein" —the thin booklet, which the young people use during their Sunday evening meetings.

The title of the "Thick Book" reads:

Ausbund
das ist
Etliche schöne
Christliche Lieder,
Wie sie in dem Gefängnis zu Passau in dem
Schloss von den Schweizer-Brüdern und
von anderen rechtgläubigen Christen
hin und her gedichtet worden.
Allen und jeden Christen,
Welcher Religion sie seien, unpartheiisch sehr
nützlich.
Nebst einem Anhang von sechs Liedern.
13. Auflage.
Verlag von den Amischen Gemeinden
in Lancaster County, Pennsylvania
1955[7]

("Selection   That is: a few beautiful Christian songs as they were now and then made in the prison in Passau in the castle by Swiss Brethren and a few other orthodox Christians. To each and every Christian, of whatever religion, impartially and useful. Be-

136

sides an appendix of six songs. 13. edition. Published by the Amish districts in Lancaster County, Pennsylvania, 1955.")

The *Ausbund* hymns have an immediate appeal in their sincerity and Christian conviction. With humility and simple forthrightness they reveal trust in God and encourage steadfastness and perseverance until the end of earthly days. Two other characteristics pervade the hymnal: the praise or defense of some particular element of faith and the memorialization of the personal suffering and tragedy of the Anabaptists, who dare to follow a new direction in religious matters. Although the writers of these songs—simple, groping men—did not often long survive their newly won positions, their doctrines and convictions have endured.

The horizon of religious truth in these hymns is circumscribed; they appeal rather to the heart than to the head. The text rambles, and the statement of simple Christian doctrine extends through repetitious and even monotonous stanzas. The congregation cannot finish any one hymn and limits itself to singing a few selected strophes. The undue length, reiteration, and vagueness of the hymns may be ample reasons why they have not been accepted outside the Amish faith.

To this day the Amish are a rather taciturn and stern, but nevertheless a robust and convinced group, of Western Christians. The hymns they sing give strong witness to the simplicity of their faith and also to the strength and endurance of their cause. The Amish believe that, should they abandon these historic expressions of their forefathers' testimony, their own group culture would likewise soon be doomed.

A cursory examination of the *Ausbund* reveals the exceeding length of most hymns: the 140 poems within the body of the book have an average of 16.4 stanzas. When the six ballads of the Appendix are added, the average rises to 17.6 stanzas per poem. The longest one in terms of

stanzas is No. 1 of the Appendix, which in 75 four-line stanzas narrates the apocryphal Old Testament story of Tobias. This story is a favorite of the Amish. The only Bible story which contains a marriage rite, it is told in prose at every wedding service. The Amish adhere strictly to the meager details given in it, and the wedding service culminates with the narration of its content.

A longer hymn, with a total number of 445 lines divided into 35 stanzas of 13 lines is No. 3 of the main text of the *Ausbund*. According to its superscription, "This is a very beautiful and comforting song about the constancy of dear, faithful Christians, which they proved for Christ's sake in all kinds of martyrs." In each stanza one of the tyrants of history is contrasted with a well-known Christian martyr.

Both of these long poems are ballads in the best tradition of this art form, and yet the former is in the rather sing-song, easy, narrative four-line stanza, alternating between the iambic masculine tetrameter and the iambic feminine trimeter. The latter, on the other hand, is in an artistic "Meisterlied" fashion of two bars of two iambic masculine tetrameters and one iambic feminine trimeter to each stanza. The "Abgesang" of each stanza is characterized by alternating iambic masculine tetrameters and feminine trimeters leading into three masculine tetrameters, of which the first and third rhyme. For oral presentation the former ballad with its uniform rhythm excels the latter with its finely worked but hard-hitting sermonizing end rhymes.

With these excessively long poems must be contrasted the shortest hymn in the book, No. 130, "O Herr nicht stolz ist mein Herz doch" ("O Lord, not proud is my heart"), a paraphrase of Psalm 130. It has only three stanzas of four lines each. This is, however, a singular example. This hymn holds closely to the biblical text, whose theme is the rest of the soul in the Lord. The three verses of the original have been turned into three quatrains with a fine feeling for the original mood. It is an excellent example of a vernacular rendering of an ancient Hebrew psalm and can stand comparison with the best of such Protestant adaptations.

A summary of the number of lines per stanza shows the following: 3 lines per stanza in 1 hymn; 4 lines in 19; 5 lines in 15; 6 lines in 11; 7 lines in 28; 8 lines in 38; 9 lines in 12; 10 lines in 5; 12 lines in 4; 13 lines in 10; 16 lines in 1; 20 lines in 1; and 33 lines in 1 hymn.

Throughout the *Ausbund* the iambic rhythm predominates, culminating for the most part in couplets of four and three feet. The masculine or accented verse is preferred over the feminine or unaccented ending. This seems to lend firmness, manliness, and strength to the expressions of these believers in a new cause. Persecution and death were able to still the voice of the singers but not the doctrines for which they gave their energy.

A surprising similarity prevails in any given pattern of stanzas. For instance in the nineteen hymns of four-line stanzas, only two variations of end rhymes occur, namely *aabb* or *abab*. In the twenty-eight hymns of seven lines, the stanzas are distinctly divisible into two halves, with a few exceptions. The first half has invariably the four-line rhyme *abab* and the conclusion has either a *ccd* or *cdc* pattern. There is no variation in the five hymns of ten lines, and ten of the twelve nine-line poems show identical patterns. It is especially in the longer stanzas that one might expect to find a rich growth of imaginative versification; this does not occur. It is therefore not only the excessive length of the song which makes for monotony; the repetitive sameness of metrical arrangements undoubtedly adds its share.

Analysis of the structure of the stanzas of the *Ausbund* reveals that the Anabaptist hymnographers, although most of them came from the shops of the cities, were not inventive rhymesters.

Textual scrutiny shows that many of the hymns are original creations; some can definitely be traced to previous lyric forms. A few of the Anabaptist hymnwriters must have belonged to the "Meistersinger," the master craftsmen, who

139

devoted their leisure time to the making of poetry and music. Some hymns must be classified as original "Meister-lieder"—mastersongs. Others again were modeled after current "Meisterlieder," folksongs, watchmen's songs, travel songs, bath songs, soldiers' songs, and even "Schnadder-hüphle" (rounds). Proponents of the new Protestant faith adapted their teachings to the prevailing songs, changing only text and melody as necessary. The Anabaptist writers worked in this way too, differing in that they changed only the words to fit the given tune.

Even today the Amish do not use written notes. The melody of the hymns is briefly indicated by a reference to an old tune. Members of the Amish congregations and especially the "Vorsänger" or song leaders memorize these tunes; the male members of a district often spend considerable time and effort in such exercises. Accompanying voices and instruments are taboo. One "Vorsänger" leads in any given hymn. He intones every line and leads the whole congregation.[8] The tune itself is, however, hidden in a welter of embellishing notes. Every syllable of text has an emphatic note around which is woven an ornamental or arabesque phrase. The latter demands great vocal and memory skill on the part of the leaders, while at the same time it delays the progress of singing considerably. To the uninitiated this whole procedure sounds as if the monovoiced congregation were being pulled along slowly through a mesh of vocal gyrations. Joseph K. Yoder, a one-time member of an Amish district in Pennsylvania, in an attempt to make singing easier and to give the melodies greater permanence, provided notes to the tunes which the songleaders of his native surroundings sang for him.[9] His coreligionists, however, rebuffed these efforts, as they rejected the use of instruments or any other kind of music apart from what they had always had. Yoder's musical notations have shown, however, that musical memory is not altogether reliable and that aural tradition lends itself to change.

Already in some instances the musical embellishments

voiced in Ohio differ from those of Pennsylvania. On the other hand, an analysis of the melodies of the *Ausbund* led the musicologist, George Pullem Jackson, to conclude that many of them date back to early folksongs. He traced one as far back as the eleventh century, to the renowned "Lay of Hildebrand."[10]

The hymns of the *Ausbund* cannot serve as models of correct German. A comparison between the latest, the thirteenth American edition of 1955, and an early seventeenth-century copy reveals that the language of the *Ausbund* has not kept pace with the progress which Modern High German has made since that time. Many editors have worked on intermediate editions, but the revisers of even the recent American edition were neither poets nor philologists. It is not altogether clear whether these men were guided in their work by their own dialect, that is, their own traditional mode of thinking and speaking, or whether their devotion to a liturgical text made them forgo necessary corrections.

Some adaptations to Modern High German have been made, but differences in the spelling of certain vowel and consonant combinations are most noticeable. Much of medieval grammar and of some local influences have been preserved. Without doubt, too, through the efforts to maintain a given rhyme and rhythm pattern the language suffered. Because the *Ausbund* is now neither pure sixteenth-century nor pure twentieth-century German, the present edition of the hymnal contains amazing and fascinating mixtures comparable with no other current book. A totally new, or at least different, language has evolved.

The *Ausbund* is the Amish book. It has remained wholly in the hands of a rural people, and it must be regarded as the achievement and testimony to this sectarian mind and language. The Amish collective mind has worked on this hymnal; it has preserved what it understood, and it has molded to its own interest whatever was usable and adaptable. The first edition of the hymnbook was not comparable to their other liturgical book, Luther's German Bible, a

Das Lobsang.

K'sunge beim
Christian Z. Yoder und
Rheuben Kauffman, 1907.

(Das zweite Lied jeden Sonntag).

1. O   Gott Va — ter wir   lo — ben   dich
2. Öff — ne den Mund Herr dei — ner   Knecht,
3. Gieb un — serm Her — zen   auch Ver — stand,

Und   bei — ne Gü — te   prei — sen;
Gieb ihn'n Weis — heit dar — ne — ben,
Er — leuch — tung hie auf Er — den,

Das   du dich O   Herr gnä — dich — lich,
Das   sie dein Wort mög'n spre — chen recht,
Das   dein Wort in uns werd be — kannt,

An   uns neu haft be — wie — sen,
Was   dient zum from — men Le — ben,
Daß   wir fromm mö — gen wer — ben,

Und   haft uns   Herr zu — sam — men g'führt
Und   nütz — lich ist zu dei — nem Preis,
Und   le — ben in Ge — rech — tig — keit,

Uns   zu er — mah — nen durch dein Wort,
Gieb uns Hun — ger nach sol — cher Speis,
Ach — ten auf dein Wort al — le — zeit,

Gieb uns   Ge — nad zu die — sem.
Das   ist un — ser Be — geh — gen.
So   bleibt man un — be — tro — ren.

pure German work. The Amish do not print their own editions, and therefore the Bible remains free of their own dialect influences. They regard the biblical text as sacred. It contains not only the "Gospel Truth," the infallible word of God, but the Scriptures are further raised to a place not unlike that of sacred texts of ancient religions. The Amish show their reverence in that the whole congregation stands when the bishop or deacon reads the text. Because the Amish do not speak High German, the language of the Testaments, however, becomes less and less intelligible. The Amish are not actively in touch with Modern High German, and the use of an English version of the Bible by way of commentary on textual difficulties becomes the rule rather than the exception.

Some few Amish, however, may be said to be trilingual. The older ones speak fluent English when they appear in the outside world; they have learned it upon entering the public or parochial school. Some may comprehend High German which they read in the Scriptures. However, their daily medium with their own kind of people is a distinct form of German dialect, generally designated as Pennsylvanisch Deitsch. The *Ausbund* is dialect and High German, a mixture of older and still usable German words and grammar, unique as the Amish themselves, inseparable from their way of life. The *Ausbund* fits their costume and it is as appropriate for the Amish as a modern hymnbook for liberal Protestants. It allows the Amish to raise their voices in spiritual unity. The *Ausbund* will come increasingly into focus as the Amish people retreat further into the rural hinterland of America.[11]

CHAPTER VI

AMISH LIFE AS REVEALED IN THE
SUGARCREEK *BUDGET*

The Sugarcreek "Budget"

Week after week the Sugarcreek *Budget*,[1] the Amish newspaper, shatters conventional ideas of journalism. It has, for
instance, no headlines, no front-page news, national nor international. It has no political analysts, no nationally renowned columnists. It has no editorial page, no back page
illustrated with pictures, no sports news, apart from local
Sugarcreek items; neither does it have comics or cartoons
of any kind. Yet it is a standard-sized newspaper of eight to
fourteen pages.

The *Budget* is published on Thursday of every week in
Sugarcreek, Tuscarawas County, Ohio. John C. Miller
brought out the first issue on May 15, 1890, a small four-
page venture with three columns to the page. In 1959 the
paper went to seven-hundred post offices in forty-two different states and ten foreign countries. The bulk of its cir-
culation goes outside its hometown. Sugarcreek is a small
village in one of the richest agricultural sections of Ohio,

close to the counties of Holmes, Stark, and Wayne, all known for their large settlements of Mennonites and Amish. "Budget John," as the old-timers called the founder, saw the need for a newspaper of a special kind to serve the Amish population. More and more Amish were arriving in the neighborhood of Sugarcreek; at the same time they were spreading to many other localities across the country. Without a newspaper, which their religious beliefs forbade them to publish, there was little opportunity for them to keep in touch with other Amish folks and activities except by letter. Miller decided to ask the Amish to send letters to him, which he would publish, with news of themselves, their families, and neighbors. He developed a system of regular country contributors. The idea was welcomed and the practice has continued to this day, with one "scribe," man or woman, often a semi-invalid, as a regular reporter for a district. Under this system the *Budget* has become a national clearinghouse of Amish news. Its present editor and publisher, George R. Smith, not a Mennonite, continues to increase the number of readers and reporters and to become acquainted personally with every one of his correspondents.

Contrary to what one might expect, the *Budget* is published in English. Although German is the Amishman's mother tongue, the spelling of his dialect, which he has no chance to see in print, would baffle him. Nevertheless the German way of turning a phrase leaves its imprint upon the style of the Amish writers, as will be seen later.

The Amish newpaper has gone through many hands, locations, types, and formats, but its readers and "scribes" have remained loyal to the paper as well as to Old Order beliefs and ways of doing things, loyalties that at first may have seemed contradictory. Indeed one of the remarkable accomplishments of the editors of the *Budget* is to have convinced the Amish to support the venture, which they do both by their subscriptions and their reports. Not taboo, the *Budget* serves the general interests of the Amish sect, for it helps maintain the strength of vital family ties in the face of widespread Amish dispersion throughout America. Weekly reports of ordinary events as well as of special occurrences of general importance are recorded in the paper and read by families and friends separated by the search for land. A brief note or sometimes a detailed account to the *Budget* is the quickest way to let everyone know whom the travelers have seen, who has driven them, where they have stayed, how long they have visited with various families, and what their future moves will be. Naturally, the travelers inform all their past hosts of their safe arrival and do not fail to thank them and to invite them in turn. Thus the *Budget* acts as an economical and regular means of communication among the various settlements. Through the *Budget*, too, the lay world receives indirectly a glimpse into the retired, quiet, and humble nature of these people.

Because of the paucity of family names among the Amish, the *Budget* is careful to record the middle initial, which every Amish man and woman takes from the first letter of the father's Christian name. In large families like the Millers, Yoders, or Troyers, sometimes the initial of the grandfather's first name must be added in order to distinguish descendants.

One learns here that the good old biblical names are still common with the Amish but are in competition with modern or more euphonious ones. The names of the children of large families are often a study in contrasts. In one family there are, for example, Benjamin, Samuel, Isaac, Stephen, John, Israel, Christ, Barbara, Mary, Hannah, Annie, Mattie, and Lizzie. Another family has chosen these names for its children: Sarah, Lizzie, Samuel, Benjamin, John, Annie, Marie, Daniel, David, Enos, Sylvia, and Malinda. Then there are three Amish brothers named Isaac, Levi, and Elmer. One wonders how Vesta, Delila, Dena, Saloma, Drusilla, or Verba, or boys' names like Junie, Venus, or Aquilla came into strict Christian families?

No Amish family or community, no matter how removed it may be, needs feel itself forgotten as long as the United

States mail service can reach it. The *Budget* is delivered sometimes to places which the general reader would be unable to find on a map—isolated communities or simply post office stations.

Consciously, and more often unconsciously and artlessly, much of Amish life reveals itself in the *Budget*. One must also agree with one Amish subscriber who was frank to remark that the the *Budget* is his weekly comic book, fascinating and humorous even without pictures. In their simplicity and homeliness the reports of the scribes give a faithful representation of the people. What concerns them most, what is uppermost in their hearts and minds, what is going on within their limited surroundings—these things one finds revealed in the Amishman's own peculiar manner. The announcements about the weather, what the men and women are doing, who preached, for example, in "Lower Pequea North East," where the service was held in "Upper Middle Pequea North" (and indeed "Eli, Christ and Mary . . . came to dinner one Sunday"), who is in the hospital, who had an accident, who was born or died, who was married, who attended, as "witnesses or hostlers," who joined the church—all this and more one finds in the columns of the weekly gazette.

Some reporters are frank to state, for example: "It has been a long time since I have written to the *Budget*, so I will try and write a few lines for our newsy paper." "Thanks to . . . for being the Budget-scribe from Kansas, as I had often wished someone would do their bit from there." "It wonders me whether the snow was too deep at Conowango so that the mailman couldn't get the scribe's news to the post office." Personal jibes and good-natured teasing such as, "New Wilmington scribe, wake up," are not missing and bring forward prompt answers. Replies to queries are often of an individual nature, as may be seen from this one: "——— wrote a few weeks ago that he did not have time to write because their baby was so 'griddlich.' Poor, innocent child, must have inherited it from his prominent 'pop.'

148

Keep on writing ———." The answer followed soon: "To ———, I think our baby got its 'hollering' habits from its numerous Pequea-er friendshoft, or at least I have mine all yet."

The cycle of the seasons and the accompanying work in homes and field have predominant importance for rural people. There is no end to such announcements as these, in the characteristic Amish manner: "We were having more winter weather with some real cold blustery days." "Some people scoff at almanac signs. To observation, whenever a Hershel occurs, there is generally a cold 'snap.' One had been again this time." "Had only what we called skiffs of snow all winter." "Today first day of Spring was nice and ideal wash day." "The men are sowing oats, and women are planting gardens and truck patches." "Nice weather and people are making good use of it, too. Sowing oats is in full swing. Some are done. Plowing for corn is on the go too. Some gardens are plowed, and women are busy at planting and cleaning house." "Was quite wet, which stopped some plowing through here." "Strawberry pickers have started picking up." "Hope the old German saying will become true: 'En druckener Marz, nasser Abril und en kuehler Maie bringt fiel frucht und haie' " ["A dry March, wet April, and a cool May bring much fruit and hay"]. "Memorial day . . . much money foolishly spent." "Today is uneasily warm." "Corn looks real good for this time of the year, so do the weeds." "Apples and peaches are plentiful and the Schwartz cider will made its first run August 11th." "Women are busy canning peaches, corn and tomatoes and getting the school clothes ready." "The hum of silo filling can be heard in many directions these days." "Farmers are busy cutting corn, filling silos, sowing wheat, digging potatoes, and what not." "Equinox brought us no unpleasant conditions."

"The men are cutting corn and hunting squirrels." "Weather was still very summerish." "It is quite dry and if it should winter up under such conditions, wells and streams will suffer. Early sowing is nice, as well as barley." "We already had a real rabbit snow." "We've had our first snow on the 27th. Some say this means we are due for 27 snows this winter." "Farmers are butchering and attending sales and weddings." "Quite a few a-butchering this week. Hence not so many weddings a-going." "Rather unusual weather for the wedding season. Five were held on Tuesday. Many more on Thursday—some said ten, but personally I doubt if there were that many. If there were that many, it would be a record number for a single day." "The men are rounding up the deer trails and crossings with high fever." "All nature is confirming the truthfulness of the Holy Word that while the earth remains summer and winter and heat and cold shall not cease."

After the weather, nothing seems of such importance to these men of the soil as health. Sickness and accidents are frequent items of Amish news: "I hope the Editor and the *Budget* readers will excuse me for not writing so long, as my husband had a bad heart condition and is still in bed most of the time. The writer also has a very bad cough." "Since so many friends are wondering how my wife is getting along and it takes so much writing to write them all, I will take this way to let them know." "We trust the above-named writer will submit a complete account of the baby's illness and death." Many contributors, as the last example suggest, ask for information about the health of members of other communities.

Many of these write-ins are extremely detailed. Thus, one can learn that the Amish are afflicted with whooping cough, mumps, measles and chicken pox, rheumatic heart, rheumatic fever, colds, upset stomachs, summer complaint and bowel trouble, nerves, flu, pets or felon on fingers, skin rash, boils, proud flesh, poison on foot or arm, lung fever, epileptic spells, and "pus on the kidneys." One also finds that "Mrs. ——— had 28 teeth extracted"; "Mrs. ——— wants to have teeth pulled tomorrow"; "——— spits blood that drains from the head"; "——— was kicked in the stomach by a horse and has not been so well for a few days"; "——— goes

to the hospital for a course of intravenous feeding." The language of these reports is always plain: "——— is kept under dope a good bit of the time." One scribe concludes his news: "I am affected with a bad cough and my wife has the grippe again."

There are many exact accounts of particular afflictions or unusual happenings. One correspondent begins: "The reason I am writing is because so many friends and relatives are wondering how we got dog fleas in the house and how we found out." After an explicit narration about treatments with various doctors and specialists, he concludes: "I am thanking each and every one who tried to help us in any way, and those who visited us during those long restless hours." One long account relates the discovery of tuberculosis: "On Saturday evening, May 7, I had a bad hemorrhage. It started from a light cough." The discussion of the fate of a Kansas housewife who came into the house one cold morning from milking the cows and tried to "pep up" a fire of green cottonwood with kerosene continued through many editions of the *Budget*. Then there are detailed descriptions, for example, of a girl who gets epileptic fits, of a boy who had all the symptoms and treatments of diphtheria, of appendectomies and operations for ruptured spleens. Some are so exact that neither hour and minutes nor number of stitches are omitted.

Kicks by horses are familiar *Budget* items. The high-spirited buggy horses are an ever-present source of danger. The catastrophes range from broken jaws to broken ribs, and one boy had to have silver plates put into the side of his head to replace the broken bones. The Amish buggy seems in no way safer than the modern automobile when it comes to accidents, and all, young and old, male and female, may be affected.

Collisions between automobiles and horse-drawn vehicles seem to be increasing. One older scribe considered it necessary to devote a whole column to precautions directed to his "horse and buggy" readers. Not only are the horses and buggies frequently demolished, but the riders as well.

Then one reads about the ever-recurring farm accidents—sawing off a thumb, catching a hand or finger in a meat grinder, or breaking bones in falls off a wagon, out of the haymow, or out of the barn door. Worse are sawmill or silage shredder accidents, or gorings by bulls. Tragedy often seems to visit the Amish community, especially its children.

The Amish farmers, while they are not opposed in principle to treatment by doctors, hospitals, and modern drugs, seem inclined to believe in patent medicines and quack cures. Doctors are often called only as a last resort, though they are regarded with special esteem. This is shown by the solicitude of the Amish farmer whose place was flooded and who had to row the doctor across his land. For the doctor's comfort he put his best rocking chair into the rowboat. Amish women have also come to like the convenience of modern hospital care, especially in confinement cases. However, the nurses of a private community hospital had considerable trouble with husbands who insisted on sleeping with their wives, regardless of the other patients in the room, because they had never slept without them. It took practically the whole hospital staff to persuade the men to a different course.

Two rare glimpses into Amish life mention "rheumatic health rings" and the apparently good effect they have upon rheumatic heart patients. These "rings" are "magnetic" steel bands, worn on one finger. They supposedly draw impurities out of the blood. They look like wedding rings but are not, of course, since wedding rings are not allowed. Questioned by the author about the efficacy of his magnetic ring, one Amishman pointed to the discoloring of the finger around the ring as convincing proof of the poison extracted from his system. Incidentally, his wife wore a ring as a precaution against rheumatism. For opposite reasons, the Amish do not smoke cigarettes. The frequent discoloration on the fingers of those indulging is sufficient proof of their poisonous nature. Cigars, stogies, or the small variety, "Between the Acts," show no such obvious evil.

The great number of advertisements of cure-alls and health panaceas in the *Budget* indicate that they find ready purchase by the Amish. The paper carries a never-ending array of ads for oils, salves, minerals, compounds, herbs, lotions, health foods, and other medicines, as well as the customary advice by "specialists." Many of these nostrums are for humans, but just as many are for livestock and some are proclaimed efficacious for either. Patent medicines which claim to cure ailments as diverse as arthritis, neuritis, rheumatism, nervousness, heart condition, blood pressure, spring fever, and, in fact, every conceivable ailment including cancer receive wide notice. Cures for ruptures and piles need no special mention, but they do have the largest advertisements. The true confessions of a scribe who fell for a certain such line of "advice" show a quiet sense of humor. "Someone," she writes, "gave the advice to use a mixture of salt and corn meal, half of each, for a dry shampoo. Rub well into the hair, then brush out. I tried it, being curious, of course, as to what the result would be and now I do consider 'mush flour' in the mouth better than in the hair, although it may be ideal for men." A well-known and often applied home remedy is the dung poultice. One can imagine the horror of the modern medical man who was called to an Amish home and found the woman of the house completely wrapped in a fresh cow dung poultice after a miscarriage. Nothing but certain death was his prediction. His shock was doubled when a week later he saw the same woman rocking herself happily on the sunny porch of her house.

The *Budget* also brings explicit accounts and testimonies by witnesses of instantaneous healings caused by anointments. One such write-up reads in part:

> We could not let any more people in on account of my heart. The anointing service began at two-thirty.

We had scripture reading, prayer, and singing. We also confessed our faults one to another, although no one had any secret sins to confess. After another season of prayer, in which all present were asked to take part, Brother . . . anointed me in the name of Jesus Christ. They had prayer again. I felt that I was healed immediately. However, I still debated whether I should arise while my company was still present or wait until they went home. They were still singing, and I asked them to sing the doxology, which became my praise song. While they were singing, I asked for my shoes, sat up and put them on, and walked over and sat on a dining room chair—something I had been unable to do for nine or ten months. I was completely healed!

In connection with illnesses one notices the many generous announcements of "dime or dollar or whatever anyone wishes to send" showers. The announcements may read in part like these: "——— to Mrs. ———. She was in the hospital for a serious operation Sept., 1948, and was in the hospital again March, 1949, when their baby was born, and maybe she will have to go again. I know it is badly needed. They have eight children and she can't work any. . . ." "——— has a large family. He has been deaf since childhood. His daughter is undergoing treatment away from home, and his third son was kicked by a horse several years ago and has lost the sight of one eye and his face is disfigured that they have to operate. It will be a serious operation but must be done to save the boy future trouble. . . ."

Announcements of these showers bear results to judge from the cards of thanks which usually follow. The sum of money received is only rarely mentioned. An eighty-year-old woman who recovered from a stroke thanked her friends in Michigan, Oregon, Illinois, Florida, Maryland, Indiana, Pennsylvania, Virginia, and Missouri for "seventy-four greeting cards, $34.95 in money, and the good eats." One recipient thanks for an "English Bible," many greetings, letters, a "nice" amount of money, handkerchiefs, peaches, cake, and ice cream. The boy mentioned in the preceding paragraph who needed the facial operation received "162 get-well cards and $136 in money, and many nice gifts from other people. The Green School and the Sandhill School each made up a sunshine box for him. He took great pleasure in opening these boxes."

THE OBITUARIES

The *Budget* gives much space and play to obituaries. They belong to the weekly news. Every student of the Amish knows that these people present a close-mouthed, taciturn manner to those outside their group. In startling contrast are these accounts of circumstances which surround the death of one of their members. Their pent-up emotions and restraint find release in the lengthy, if seemingly maudlin accounts which oddly enough always culminate in poetic or rhymed conclusions. Special interest centers, therefore, on these items of the *Budget*.

In the obituaries, as nowhere else in Amish society, one finds recorded the full name of the deceased, with maiden name of the woman, names of parents and grandparents, maiden names of mother and grandmother, and the exact number of years, months, and days the person had lived; in addition, here are also the names and locations of all children and brothers and sisters, with married names if necessary, and such honest comments as "one son, whereabouts unknown."

Excerpts from the *Budget* read as follows: ". . . died of heart attack at the age of 68 years, 5 months, 19 days; lived in matrimony 47 years, 4 months, 1 day, had 9 children, 3 of whom preceded him in death. He leaves to mourn 57 grandchildren of whom 43 are living, and 2 great grandchildren." A certain bishop, 89, the oldest man to die during 1949, left this amazing progeny: 270 descendants, including

7 sons, 7 daughters, 105 grandchildren, and 151 great grand-children. The *Budget* item continues: "Additional survivors are his wife, 2 stepsons, 2 stepdaughters, 4 sisters and 1 brother." At this man's funeral twenty-two ministers, all related directly or indirectly to the deceased, with six bish-ops in the group, participated. His aged widowed sisters, 86 and 87, and his brother, 84 years old, also attended.

In contrast with this long-lived patriarch appeared a no-tice of the death of a child, "1 month, 6 days, who left to mourn his parents, 2 grandfathers, 2 grandmothers, 1 great grandfather, 3 great grandmothers, 6 uncles, 6 aunts, and many friends and relatives." In a similar instance, a girl of 2 years, 1 month, 23 days, left to mourn "father, mother, 2 brothers, 1 sister, 2 grandfathers, 2 grandmothers, 2 great grandfathers and 1 great great grandmother, 6 uncles, 14 aunts and a host of other relatives and friends. One sister preceded her in death 18 months ago."

No mention is made as a rule of stillborn infants, but a story like the following is not uncommon: "Mrs. Malinda ——— died in an ambulance on the way to the hospital after the birth of a child a few hours before. The child is well. She is survived by her bereaved husband and 8 children, 7 boys and 1 girl, the oldest nearly 14 years. Also her aged mother and 6 sisters and 1 brother who also saw his dear life companion laid in her grave 2 years ago with 10 chil-dren left behind."

After the death of husband or wife, remarriage is an al-most invariable rule. One item in the *Budget* vouches for this implicitly with an account of a preacher who during the first thirteen years of his married life had seven sons and four daughters; his second wife brought him seven children from a previous marriage, and they had one son of their own union of nine years; a third wife, with whom he lived seven more years brought along six children of her own. This man was therefore father and stepfather to twenty-five children. Similarly all widows seem to remarry if they have unmarried children, and all orphans are taken into families within the

Amish community. Orphanages and old people's homes are unknown.

After reading the *Budget* columns carefully for a year, one becomes conscious not only of the large families of the Amish but also of the accompanying large number of deaths among these people. The recorded deaths may be classed in three groups: hardly a family avoids losing an infant; men and women in their early thirties; and the older group in the late sixties, seventies, and eighties. Infant mortality is high because children come into the family so frequently and, in part, because the Amish try home cures before they call the doctor and, again, because mother is so busy with her daily chores she cannot possibly give adequate care and attention to all illness in early stages.

A summary account from the *Gospel Harold*, a weekly Mennonite publication, reprinted in the January 5, 1950, issue of the *Budget*, lists 543 deaths for all Mennonites, not separating the Amish, as reported to it in 1949. Of these 291 were males and 252 were females. Among the men were 6 bishops, 10 ministers, and 8 deacons. Nearly 54 per cent, or 289, exceeded the allotted time of three score and ten years. The average age was 64 years, one month and one day. The analysis showed the number of deaths occurring as follows:

By Ages		By Months	
Under 1 year:	27	Jan.:	43
1— 9:	16	Feb.:	36
10—19:	10	Mar.:	63
20—29:	15	Apr.:	45
30—39:	14	May:	66
40—49:	29	June:	39
50—59:	57	July:	41
60—69:	80	Aug.:	38
70—79:	150	Sept.:	39
80—89:	122	Oct.:	45
90—99:	25	Nov.:	47
100— :	1	Dec.:	41

Pennsylvania led with nearly 32 per cent, or 172 deaths, followed by Ohio with 16 per cent, or 87; Indiana, 47; Illinois, 32; Virginia, 29; Iowa, 27. Many other states and provinces of Canada had less than twenty. These latter figures may also be taken as indicative of the relative strength of Mennonite populations in these states.

The causes of death follow national trends, with the Amish frequent victims of heart trouble caused by rheumatic fever. Modern diseases have also invaded Amishland: cancer, encephalitis, meningitis, Hodgkin's disease, uremic poisoning, cerebral hemorrhage, strokes, peritonitis, measles followed by pneumonia, ulcers. One woman reportedly died of "heart trouble, dropsy and diabetes." Many of these reports indicate that the Amish avoid medical treatment until critical illness attacks the victim, with little preventive care among the people. Often the patient is taken to a doctor only after home remedies and patent medicines have failed. Accidental deaths take a large toll. Every year has its share of drownings, burns, fatal collisions with automobiles. One two-and-a-half-year-old child fell out of the high chair with a resultant "rupture of the brain," as the *Budget* scribe described it.

Funerals in Amishland become community rites with visitors from the deceased person's own group. One account from Virginia mentions that "guests were present from Iowa, Illinois, Indiana, Ohio, Pennsylvania, Delaware and several regions of Virginia." At another funeral someone was impressed sufficiently by the multitude to count the mourners and found by actual count "466 or 467, which, with relatives made over 500." With such crowds the following line in an obituary seems plausible: "Last Tuesday was the funeral of ——— with a large attendance. It was held in the broiler house."

The conclusion of the Amish obituaries shows a sentimental tendency in these people, as they invariably end with a poem or jingle of four to twenty lines. Perhaps Johann Gottfried Herder was right when he said that poetry was the language of primitive people. The Amish, simple and unlettered as they are, cling to flowery, sweet verses as a proper way to express their feelings about death. The poems certainly are not original, the lines are borrowed and are merely adapted to the particular situation at hand. One would expect the Amish to express themselves in the language they know best, in which they would have a certain rhyming facility. That is, however, not the case. Although German is their everyday language, German rhymes seldom occur and only when the one mourned was an older person. Because they are signed, the rhymes seem to be the compositions of the respective signers. Casual comparison, however, disproves such originality, apart from that exercised in substituting and rearranging a couplet or a word here and there. Certain clichés have found particular favor and are often woven into the poem. Demarcation by stanzas is practically unknown.

In the following examples the words in parentheses do actually occur but are changed with each obituary. First names often appear within the lines without regard to rhythm. The verse may easily be adapted to the situation in question, as the following lines will show:

> One long year has passed away since that sad day
> When dear (Malinda) passed away. . . .

> . . . Oh, (Clara), how we miss you
> From our eyes tears often flow,
> For you are always with us
> Though you left us (four) year ago.

> . . . God only knows how we miss you
> At the end of the (second) year. . . .

> . . . (Joni) is dead, the sad story is told,
> He died as a baby while others grow old. . . .

(Two) years ago today
God peacefully called away
(Brother Jones), loved by all,
'Twas a heartbreaking call. . . .

. . . It was in the month of June
On (Sunday the twelfth)
When (Esther) was called so soon
And left us by ourselves.

After such initial statements follows the much repeated couplet:

Oh, how sad was the day
When dear (Esther) was called away. . . .

In the following stanza the first word may readily be exchanged with father, mother, brother, or sister:

(Grandmother) was tired and weary,
Weary with toil and with pain.
Put by (her) glasses and rocker
(She) will not need them again. . . .

Occasionally within a poem these consoling verses are found:

. . . All is dark within our dwelling,
Lonely are our hearts today,
For the one we loved so dearly
Is not dead, he is just away. . . .

The last line often shows the variant: "Is now gone away. . . ." Other lines expressing sentiments which seem to appeal to compositor and relatives alike and in which only the pronouns need changing to suit any case are:

(She) was always kind and loving
And we all loved (her) so well. . . .

We loved (her), Oh perhaps too well
For soon (she) slept and died.

In the following two pairs of lines, the beginning and the end rhymes have been preserved, but the rest is often changed:

... Oh, how I longed for more words from you
But all in vain, except a few....

... Oh, how I longed to talk and shake hands with you
But alas, you were gone too.

Confusion seems to exist whether the following lines should read "with" or "without." Both versions occur, mainly referring to mother but occasionally also to father or parents:

    ... What is a home (without) a mother,
    A tender oft repeated thought,
    Yet we know not half the meaning
    Until by experience taught....

Bereaved parents seem to be especially fond of expressing their feelings in the following manner.

Dear little hands, we miss them so!
All through the day, wherever we go!
All through the night how lonely it seems,
For no little hands wake us out of our dreams....

Here again the first line in this group may be made to read: "Dear little hands, I miss them so," or, with a name inserted, "Dear little (Edna), I miss you so." Rarely do the verses grow lyrical, as they do in this instance:

Now the moon and stars are shining
    Upon his lonely grave,
Where sleeps my dear (husband),
    I loved but could not save....

Sweet little angel! How we'd have loved to keep her,
But we know God needs some pure fragrant buds
To make his kingdom complete.

These latter thoughts were expressed about a "tiny baby who spent her time in an incubator." The following apologetic lines at times conclude the parting words of a mourning wife. But they are also found given by "parents" or "the family":

> Friends may think we have forgotten,
> When at times they see us smile,
> But they little know the heartache,
> That the smile hides all the while.

Part of one poem certainly may have applied to some young person, but it seems inappropriate when applied to a 64-year-old mother of five sons and four daughters. It reads:

> The fairest lilies are the first to fall
> The sweetest first to fade.
> The fondest, dearest, best of all
> Within the grave is laid. . . .

The following description referring to an Amish father also seems rather incongruous when one considers the patriarchal and "papa is all" position in the Amish family:

> (Father), you were mild and lowly
> Gentle as the summer breeze,
> Pleasant as the air of evening
> When it floats among the trees. . . .

Old Greek mythology also finds a remnant in these often quoted lines:

> Just across the shining river
> Father landed on the shore. . . .

One of the few poems that seems original as far as the first eight and last three lines are concerned may be quoted in full because it reveals a family narrative. However, the body of the work is a compilation of the customary sentimental clichés:

Softly and peacefully she passed away
In an ambulance to be taken to the hospital,
    but did not stay,
Soon her dead body was again brought home
To be laid away in her silent tomb.
I think of the sorrow this brother had,
To go home to his children who were all in bed,
To tell them the sad news their dear mother is gone
And seemed so lonely to be left alone.
    The Lord has ways we don't understand
    But he is ever ready with a helping hand,
    To help the dear ones that are in need,
    So think of that comfort and do not grieve.
    So farewell, companion and children dear,
    Do not shed for me many a tear.
    I hope you all will faithful be,
    Prepare to die and follow me.
    Farewell, dear mother, brother and sisters all.
    It was the Lord's will, he made the call.
    My time was here, the Lord knows best,
    To take us home and give us rest.
    The home circle is broken, but now started
        in heaven,
    For the dear ones that are left behind.
    Father and children, 7 small boys in number,
    And only one daughter, Katie, is left behind
    To feel the loss of a dear mother.
                        By an Aunt ———

From reading these lengthy sentiments in honor of their departed members, one must conclude that the Amish feel instinctively that the language used to speak to or address their dead must be of an exalted vein, "gehobene Sprache," as the German defines poetry. One likewise senses in lines which become trite by constant repetition that the Amish stand here, upon the death of one of their number, before an ever-recurring mystery which becomes less awesome by the use of rhymed and scanned language. There exists no sense of regret or shame for borrowing this poetry from unknown creative sources. Death thus becomes less a tragedy than it is a test of the Amish belief in the wisdom of God's unknowable ways. Though the "home circle may be broken," the Amish nonetheless recognize unquestionably and unshakably the "Lord's will." The human incidents only go to heighten the quiet acceptance of destiny, immortality, and reunion in the other world.

Newsworthy Items

A reading of the *Budget* supplies miscellaneous news items of casual interest: "Some young folks enjoyed an evening with Miss Mary ——— at Ben ———'s"; or "Fanny ——— helps to do the chores at Ezra ———'s during the absence of them." "Had church service at Enos ———'s. Forty-five were present. Sermon by Enos ———. He is putting down cement walks around his house."

Reporters comment on preachers and sermons only rarely. Occasionally a notice compliments the good sermon of visiting preachers—"the two ministering brethren brought us Spirit-filled messages." One must remember that many Mennonites and all Amish believe not only in the verbal inspiration of the Bible but also in the guidance of the holy Spirit in their leaders. Therefore, their preachers do not need a special education beyond the ability to read the Bible. One Amish contributor to the *Budget*, indeed, wrote a long article against the modernization that is slowly creeping into the Amish church and how it is following the "popular trends of modern religion." He maintained: "We can see it and hear it everywhere, yes, even in the columns of the *Budget*, much as we regret to admit it." Among the many points of complaint he lists the "educated ministry trained in worldly wisdom, philosophy, sociology, public speaking, etc." These things are for him the "serpent trying to deceive us even as he deceived Eve."

It must have been coincidence that in one congregation in Pennsylvania the Sunday services were conducted by a bishop and a preacher both of whose first names were Christ. Of the bishop it is further said: "Christ seems very good for his age, and is busy every day doing carpenter work for people near home." An unusual *Budget* item occurred in the brief biography of a member of their sect: "He was a preacher for 75 years; during all this time he never accepted one cent for his labor. He performed 3,000 marriages, baptized 5,000 persons and preached 5,000 funeral sermons. He never was on a railroad train. He made his living off his little farm. He left 12 children, 50 grandchildren, 50 great-grandchildren, and 5 great-great-grandchildren. He was born on a Thursday, was married three times on a Thursday, was converted on Thursday, and died on a Thursday." The announcement of the birth of a "baby girl at the 11th minute of the 11th hour, on the 11th day of November, 1949" certainly was meant for those interested in horoscopes.

The *Budget* often discusses in its columns the scarcity of land which is plaguing the Amish more and more. They are forced to disperse to distant, remote parts of the nation. There is hardly an Amish community that has not experienced the loss of members through removal. As one contributor from Pennsylvania puts it: "A good bit of moving will be done the next weeks [i.e., in Spring], with a good many people moving out of the valley because farms just cannot be gotten here; it seems to be full everywhere, and being walled in with mountains much like the cities of ancient times, we cannot expand like other settlements. There are many young people here, married a number of years, who still are not able to get on a farm."

These farmers have their eyes on three things when they start a settlement: fairly level land, good buildings, and small rural schools. Concerning the first two points another contributor shrewdly observed: "We prefer a place where big spacious buildings are already up and ready to occupy.

165

Many such places can be found throughout the state. Let alone the land without buildings. Good farms can be brought for much less than it would cost to erect the buildings that are on them. The old people used to say: 'The condition of the buildings tells the condition of the soil.' "

From sporadic references to Amish life of a hundred or even fifty years ago, one finds that the Amish have kept abreast of the times more than is generally acknowledged. One scribe bemoans the "almost fathomless inventions" which put us "in a period the same as that of the 120 years in Noah's time." But no writer can be found who would want to revert to a time before these innovations were made. In fact, another correspondent refers to the time when there were no railroads, no telegraph, no electricity, no coal oil or glass lamps, no drills, no hay rakes, no washing machines, no mowers, no reapers, no threshing machines, to a time when everything had to be done by hand and sickles, by spinning wheel and hand needle, and when travel was either on foot or horseback. The writer only reminds his readers that the forefathers did live harder lives, with "more cross-bearings."

In the Thursday, December 15, 1949, edition of the *Budget*, a scribe announced a new bus route through the Amish territory in Wayne County, Ohio, and tells of other possible connections into Amish settlements, saying, "I hope the public [which can only be his own Amish neighbors] will patronize it enough that it will be a paying proposition." Then he concludes with these remarkable words: "It is a great convenience when you can board a bus in the morning and go to the county seat and have several hours' time to transact business and be home in time for dinner." These are most unusual words coming from the Amish because, so far, as a group they have stoutly objected to motor vehicle transportation. They will not let their children ride school busses.

Another unrelated incident shows how inroads of modern

America are invading Amishland. "There is to be a 'goin on' called a housewarming, at ——'s home tomorrow evening. Quite a few are invited. It's a new wrinkle for the Amish in this vicinity. We're told one brings a present and some cookies, which will be passed around to the guests."

Every summer lightning takes its toll of barns in Amishland. The barns are the largest buildings on the farmstead and stand unprotected by either large trees or lightning rods. The latter are taboo and cannot be erected by Amish or Old Order Mennonites. The Amish, of course, do not carry fire insurance, but the solidarity and the mutual helpfulness of the community compensate for this. The following explicit account in the *Budget* is illuminating:

> 437 volunteer helpers gathered at the barn raising on the Milo Miller farm one mile south of Walnut Creek [Holmes County, Ohio], last Thursday morning, and when evening came a brand new barn stood near the site of the one destroyed by fire Sept. 18th.
>
> The new barn, a two-story 50 × 74 foot building with 13 stanchions, three horse and four box stalls, an inside watering trough and two hay mows, was completely erected in one day. Only the basement, built of glazed tile with a concrete floor, was completed beforehand.
>
> Members of three churches—the Evangelical and Reformed, Amish and Walnut Creek Mennonite—took part in the barn raising. Miller is a member of the Walnut Creek school board and the Evangelical and Reformed Church.
>
> Men brought tools and free labor, while the women carried in hoards of ham, beef, chicken, canned goods, cake and pies, all ready to eat. A bakery truck delivered 100 loaves of bread. Ben M. Beachy and Jonas P. Miller made plans for the structure and were the building contractors. They employed about 10 men to assist Milo Miller's friends who donated their labor.

About $400 was collected from the townspeople to pay for the foundation and other preliminary work.

From this report one sees that even non-Amish neighbors with misfortunes are generously helped, as they in turn come to the assistance of the Amish. Besides the spirit of co-operation and benevolence characteristic of the Amish, their need for social intercourse finds gratification in such community undertakings; this may be seen from a similar report about a strictly Amish barn raising written by Grant M. Stoltzfus for the *American-German Review:*

Appraisers from the brotherhood met and decided on the loss which ——— sustained. Assessments according to ability to pay were made and collected from fellow members of the brotherhood. In a few days men cleared away the debris and laid the footings and foundation for the new building. The big day for the raising of the new barn was soon to come. ——— Amish families over the neighborhood anticipated the day with high rejoicing. Early in the morning the highways in all directions were filled with horses and buggies going to ———'s farm. In all, two hundred and eight horses were tied at the farmstead. At every barn raising there is a spirit of joviality and exhilaration. Conversation is lively. Orders and jokes are all spoken in the Pennsylvania German dialect. At noon there was a pause as the five hundred and sixty-nine men lined up at the food tent to partake of the bountiful lunch which one hundred and sixty-nine women prepared. Large platters of fried chicken, noodles, sandwiches, pies, cakes, and fruit were eaten by the hard-working men. Paper brooms kept the flies chased away. . . . As the sun sank below the hills of Holmes County [Ohio] a new barn stood as a monument to neighborliness and mutual aid. . . .[2]

The folklorist too will find material for his collection in reading the *Budget*. His eye will catch the not-too-frequent accounts of "water findings." If the Amish need additional water resources on their farms, they will probably solicit the help of the "dowser" or water seeker before the drilling of the well is begun. There are no accounts of failures. Dowsing apparently is a special gift that is passed down from father to son. Only one report characterizes the seeker, as "an humble and unassuming person of a very friendly nature." The methods employed in locating water are several, differing with the individual seeker. One dowser's method, which is so accurate that he "could not have hit it more accurately if he had first dug a well," uses pliers instead of a fruit twig. "Gripping the pliers wide open into both hands, palms up, he slowly walked over the grounds. Suddenly the pliers snapped out of his hands. 'There's the stream,' he declared." This man, it is said, is even sought after by commercial firms. In another locality the "leading water seeker" uses a gold coin or ring swinging from a string inside an ordinary water tumbler. When he comes to the hidden underground source, the ring begins to move. "As many times as it swings and hits the sides of the glass, will be the estimated depth in feet of the water flow underneath." The designated depth was reached several times by this method.

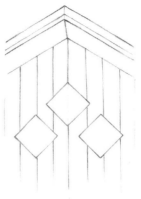

Other intimate glimpses into Amish life are at times forthcoming in the *Budget*, but much of the background is concealed. For instance, that the Amish like to ride in automobiles and are as much fascinated by them as any modern American is without question. Certain taxi drivers in towns near the Amishland can only exist because of their patronage. The *Budget* carries its share of requests for passengers or co-travelers to distant places, even to Florida. It is much greater news, however, when Amish boys are caught riding in a stolen automobile. Much explaining needed to be done in subsequent editions of the *Budget*

when it was found that a boy with the typical Amish name Schlabach, in modern dress, had taken an automobile and then had invited two other Amish youths, named Yoder and Beachy to ride along with him. All three, however, were punished upon apprehension.

More intricate, and to be sure a mere ripple on the surface of deeply stirring undercurrents, is the meager report of six Amish boys between the ages of 15 and 21 who "wanted to get even with a bishop because of differences between him and their parents." Not much else is told about the incident apart from the fact that the common pleas court of Millersburg, Holmes County, Ohio, determined that the boys "had obtained a five-gallon can of aluminum paint from the bishop and spattered it over his buggy, and also put fly spray in cattle feed. Two others obtained saws and cut down four trees at the bishop's residence." The punishment was in accordance with the crime in that the culprits had to replace the paint and the top of the buggy while the destroyed trees had to be replaced with ones of equal size which would grow for at least two years.

Politics and international affairs do not concern the other-worldly readers and contributors to the *Budget*. No "informed" Amishman, however, can do without his weekly paper if he wants to know what is happening within his own family relationship and his sectarian fold. This weekly publication has come to mean to him as much as the metropolitan newspaper means to the citizens of this world. At the same time the *Budget* unwittingly reveals the ever-increasing strain exerted upon these people by the impact of a larger and more successful economic society. Therefore, this paper pictures a people in its own peculiar setting, emphasizing its accommodation to new ways as well as its withdrawal from modern society.

CHAPTER VII

PROPAGATION OF THE PAST

COURTSHIP

The shy nature of the Amish reveals itself clearly in their manner of courting, a simple form of lovemaking which has remained unchanged through the years of rural isolation. The customs of Amish courtship, as all customs associated with the intimate lives of the Amish, may confuse modern observers, but these customs have deep roots in rural tradition.

Amish young people find few opportunities for distraction and recreation in their ascetic seclusion in the countryside. They do not frequent restaurants or snack shops, taverns or dancehalls, theaters, movies, or concert halls. Spectator pleasures, so commonplace for most American youth, have no place in the Amish scheme of living. Amish young people must find their entertainment within the family circle and at Sunday church district meetings.

Amish elders know that children need diversion and fun. They know that young people cannot completely believe that chores well done, physical energy expended on a thriving farm, or unity with the spirit of the forefathers are ample and sufficient rewards for the faithful. The Sunday evening frolic after the church service and dinner is intended to provide relaxation and enjoyment for the young people.

One of the Amish expressed his philosophy on this matter in a characteristic way: "The young folks need to work off steam, and it is better that they do it while they are young than that they should do it after they have joined the church and are married." The basic Amish method for "working off steam," of course, is to make youngsters work hard over the daily chores. But on Sunday evenings the young folks are allowed to gather in barn or house for a "singing," or "frolic." Here they sing the so-called "fast tunes" and play social games, and the young men and women have a chance to be together. A harmonica or perhaps an old-fashioned phonograph from the school provides mountain or cowboy music; only square or barn dancing is permitted, modern dancing by couples being strictly forbidden. Such frolicking stops, of course, with marriage; but, while these young people are still unbaptized and outside the church, they are allowed forms of behavior which would not be tolerated in a member.

The host, in whose house or barn the "frolic" is held, allows the young folks to remain for as long as they desire. The work of the next day in field and farm or even school seems of little concern. Everyone, including the schoolteacher, assumes that Monday is *blaue Mondag*, "blue Monday," as far as the young people are concerned.

It is during these Sunday evening occasions that a young man begins to cast his eye out for a suitable girl. When he decides on one whom he would like to accompany home, he finds a friend to intercede with the girl on his behalf. It is considered unbecoming for a young suitor to ask personally, and, in any case, his innate shyness would bar him from making a direct approach. Reticence, one of the strongest Amish characteristics, prevails here as throughout all of courtship and life. Even when a boy and girl have begun to take a strong interest in each other, they try to conceal their affection from others and to avoid the least suspicion that there could possibly be some serious thought or intention between them. To exhibit sentiment, tenderness, or passion toward another person is absolutely out of the question. It is simply unthinkable for any feeling to be exhibited, especially in the district meeting where the sexes keep severely apart. In fact the young Amish make it a purposeful game to keep all relationships with the other sex secret, even from the immediate families. This secrecy is maintained until the moment the bishop makes the announcement of the impending wedding. On this occasion the couple concerned either is not at the service or leaves before anybody else can say a word about it. The public announcement of mutual affection and of intention to marry is meant to come as a surprise to everyone.

If the boy is rejected on that first Sunday evening, he does not suffer much embarrassment or sense of rebuff since the rejection does not come to him from the girl directly. Moreover, since it would never do to let a girl harness her own horse or drive home alone in a frail vehicle along dark, country lanes, the Amish boy has further opportunities for becoming acquainted with a girl of his choice. While the Amish girl does not mind harnessing and hitching her horse, she would fret and worry about her social acceptance if she were not assisted and even escorted home. And here in the dark of the Sunday night the Amish boy may find enough courage to offer a helping hand and to show his superior horsemanship.

The demands for conformity in outward appearance would appear to leave little chance for the usual feminine or even masculine ingenuity and wiles for attracting a partner. All girls dress alike, except for the variety in the solid colors of their dresses and the skirted shirtwaist style. However, for those occasions when the authority of the disciplinarian bishops is absent, young feminine caprice finds many aids (especially in Woolworth's) which would be considered sinful and sufficient causes for excommunication in members. On the other side, except for the difference in size and figure, facial expression and color of hair, all boys seem alike. The color and cut of the serge suits, the socks and shoes, shirts and hats are the same; the neckties or striped shirts or colored socks with which the Yankee boy might want to impress his favorite are absent. But here, too, the Amish boy is a long way from the strict conformity of the Sunday morning service. One distinguishing feature of the boy, although he will scarcely admit it, is a dashing horse, perhaps with a "fancy" harness and a fine rig. He will have to remove the fanciful, polished metal or ivory adornments of the harness when he joins the church.

It would be wrong to assume that the Amish boy is wholly swayed by desire and love in the selection of his companion. It would be equally wrong to assume that it is wholly her father's good farm which makes a young woman attractive to him. No doubt "rational marriages" have occurred in Amishland. The choice of a mate and the subsequent marriage have always been considered serious affairs, regarded somewhat as business in the rural community. Marriage is indeed not child's play. In the Amish world, its tasks and labors are harder than those in other social groups. The young folks want to succeed; they must succeed economically, in spite of all the hardships which beset them. They must stay on the land, find a farm where their own children will be born and raised; they have to work in such a way that they may establish themselves eventually as a debt-free farm family.

No other event within the peasant society has grown out of the very condition of life as has the union of man and wife; no other subject, therefore, has become the focus of so much sober thought. The boy looks for "poise" in his girl; he wants her to be a "mixer," meaning that she be accepted by her own group; she expects to find in him a good worker with a robust, not slender, figure which can give testimony in work, endurance, and also ardor in his love. The young woman who is a good housekeeper, strong, healthy, considerate, alert, quick, and eager makes a valued mate. "Wie man sich bettet, so liegt man"—"as one makes one's bed, so one lies in it." This is the supreme axiom of folk wisdom concerning marriage. These considerations exceed the attractions of a fair skin and quickly fading beauty. An Amish boy does not exhibit the outward charms of his girl, just as his courtship is for the most part clandestine and concealed in darkness.

The Amish court in secrecy and under the cloak of darkness. Romance does bloom, and the ride homeward toward the girl's house is often as circuitous as possible. Visits to inns, roadhouses, taverns, or movies are out of the question. The hills, dales, and wooded lots, however, do invite lingering. By the side of a secluded lane and shady creek in the Amish country, this sign may be seen:

CARS AND BUGGIES

STAY OUT

OR ELSE

On these homeward trips the boys may be seen sitting on the girls' lap when two couples are riding together. The explanation offered is that it could not be otherwise, for how could the boys hold the reins of the horse if the girls sat on their laps? A former custom, that unmarried folks had to ride in open rigs, is no longer practical unless the father has such a vehicle left from former days and insists that his son use it.

Buggy traffic within the Amish region seems to go on throughout Sunday night until early Monday morning. No wonder that the neighbors conjecture many things. It is true, however, that the young man who takes a companion home is expected to come in and stay a while. This "while" may even extend through the whole night. The parents as a rule have secluded themselves early and safely in their own chamber, which is to the rear on the ground floor of the house. The door of an Amish home is never locked, and guests are always welcome.

Amish congregations in the past century have separated over the question of bundling. There is no proof that this protest by removal has stopped the practice inherited from olden times and from their former homeland. If one can believe writers of modern Switzerland, bundling is still practiced in the region of the Emmenthal of the Canton Bern, Switzerland, the locality from which many ancestors of the Ohio Amish emigrated. The following characterization of the present-day Bernese peasant applies very well to the Amishman of the American Midwest. Of him it is said that he is shy by nature, rather secluded, slow in making acquaintances and clumsy and stiff in social relations. To approach him in public is very difficult; he is always in fear of being laughed at and of being ridiculed. To show intimacies or any fondness for another person before strangers goes against his grain. A refusal by strangers he takes as a hurt; but the writing of letters is not his metier. Therefore he undertakes his advance skirmishes against the female sex under the protection of the nightly darkness.[1]

The conditions which prevail in Switzerland and which led to this characteristic form of lovemaking are practically unchanged in the counties of Wayne, Holmes, Coshocton, and Tuscarawas in Ohio. Here, as abroad, both the young man and woman work hard all day and all week in the barns and open hilly fields; the distances between farms, with intervening hills and valleys, are far and demand an added effort to reach the home of the favorite one; it is most natural that the young folks should recline together until daybreak. Regional environment, tradition of long standing, and the example of past generations are the conditions that justify the practice, itself a consequence both of necessity and convenience. What was said of American pioneer days may be said today: "Was it not the dictate of humanity as well as of economy, which prompted the old folks to allow the approved and accepted suitor of their daughter to pursue his wooing under the coverlid of a good featherbed rather than to have them sit up and burn out uselessly firewood and candles, to say nothing of the risk of catching their death a' cold?"[2]

The Amish do not like to commit themselves on the matter of nightly courtship, but several of their bishops have expressed views concerning it. Bishop Jacob Schwarzendruber, who in 1851 removed from Somerset County, Pennsylvania, to Johnson County, Iowa, where he had hoped to found a congregation free from bundling addressed a lengthy epistle in 1865 to the Amish ministers' conference. The bishop repeatedly bemoaned "premarital intercourse as the occasion for whoredom." He spoke frankly:

> As regards pride and pre-marital intercourse and all vices, there is much shortcoming in the discipline of children by the parents. If the ministers set them back, then the parents feel bad and even help the children to continue in vice. Experience teaches that there is a great calamity (Elend) in the church. . . . And then, how it is carried further among some, the boys go into the beds with the girls when they perhaps have drunk too much and evil consequences follow as evidenced by the dealings in the congregations and the illegitimate children are proof of it. Oh what a great sin it is, if ministers and parents and all members do not take enough care for the youth, or the mother of the house perhaps herself helps to prepare the beds. How then can the youth come to a right knowledge. I believe that if this evil which has rooted itself in all the congregations would be dealt with earnestly many young people could be brought to a knowledge of the truth which their elders desire to follow; but how sad it is that old people say, I cannot forbid this, because I myself did it. What fig leaves these are with which we try to cover ourselves, and how does this accord with a re-

pentant heart. This I write in love to all those who are willing to be warned.[3]

In Ohio Old Order Amish Bishop David A. Treyer of Holmes County expressed similar thoughts on the subject. In his *Hinterlassene Schriften*, parts of which were written in 1870 and published first in 1920, we read:

> Now we come to the unmarital lying together among the youth [one might even translate "unehe- liche Zusammenliegen" as extramarital cohabitation or simply bundling]. This is a practice, which has caused me much trouble, worry and cares in my time, because it is a thing that is in part wholly objectionable to the spirit of Christ and the word of God. Yes, it is a com- mon old custom among many confessors of Christ, an evil semblance and a great danger, especially for the untutored, lightminded youth. It is a dark light and a great disgrace before God and before many God-loving people and likewise before the world. Oh what kind of an unnecessary, dangerous exercise of the flesh! I believe to be almost convinced that in my time several faithful young souls have come thereby to sin, who perhaps in their heart had a good intention, to keep themselves chaste. It is a common proverb: "Who ex- poses himself to danger, he succumbs to danger. That is indeed often the case. . . . But now someone might think or say: Such a practice as the unmarital lying together cannot be an unfruitful work of darkness. Answer: If not, then it would have to be indeed a fruitful work of the light, or do we want to regard such things as intermediary things, which spring nei- ther from good nor from bad, and neither serve the good nor the bad. I say: No.[4]

Upon the question, "Why are such things tolerated, even approved in the community of God, as the unmarital lying together?" the Bishop later reaches the conclusion that "it is not Christian, but pagan, yes foolishness and frivolity."[5]

An Amish girl may judge her popularity by the number of suitors she has, but the girl who is known to be an easy and promiscuous prey to male advances harms her own reputation. To safeguard her own virtue and good name the wise girl soon restricts her acquaintances. On the other hand, much Amish humor plays around the circumstances of the nightly visits of the swain. The groom, on his wedding night may be reminded of the occasion when, in flight, he left the ladder outside the girl's window or was embarrassed by the removal of a buggy wheel, the harness of the horse, or even by the removal of the horse. No matter how concealed the young man may try to keep his escapades, the place, and the girl to whom he is paying his attentions, his rivals may make it their spying business to find out, to molest, and to embarrass him.

East-central Ohio has its own story of an "immaculate conception," as there is also the record of a boy's refusal to marry a pregnant girl. Upon closer examination it was found that the latter girl had been in a neighboring state when pregnancy occurred. One does not hear much about illegitimacy and promiscuity, but, if marital faithfulness and the absence of divorce are taken as indications of the absence of premarital relationship, then the Amish people stand as admirable examples. Marriage unquestionably is the most sacred and stable institution with the Amish, and the break-up of a family is practically unknown. The Amish would not tolerate in their community a betrayer and defiler of their womanhood. On the other hand, they are lenient with unmarried lovers. They have considerable respect for the wisdom of the peasant who does "not want to buy a cat in a sack." As little joking as he understands and permits about marriage, the Amishman will close an eye and even permit "a five to be an even number when it comes to lovers."

When the young people have found themselves psychologically and physically matched and are ready to establish

181

themselves as an independent family unit, they begin to think of marriage. Both know, too, that success depends on mutual hard work. "Before the empty crib, the horses bite each other" is a well-known bit of Amish wisdom. Should the male be more interested in riding through the countryside in his buggy than in work, the wife might also lose interest in her home. Their forebears have taught the couple that this earth is truly a valley of tears, that ease and comfort are not meant for this life.

In preparation for marriage the Amish youth has saved his money from the wages he received as a hired hand or day laborer, beyond his eighteenth or twenty-first birthday. Before that age, all his income went to his father, who in turn assists him with the most essential equipment, if not a complete farm. He already owns a driving horse and buggy. From his father he will receive one or two draft horses. He may have picked up a plow and harrow, aided by the judgment of his father, at a nearby auction or weekly sale. The rest of the machinery he may borrow until his establishment demands its own equipment. The girl has accumulated a chest full of household linen. If she has been hired out to work as a housemaid after the age of twenty-one, she too will have some money. Her family will also provide her with a cow and chickens and share with her their own larder. The domestic needs of the newly married couple in their own home are scant and frugal. An iron bedstead, a few chairs, perhaps even a rocking chair, a simple wooden kitchen table, which serves as dining table, a wood- or coal-burning stove or oven, a cupboard for the dishes—that is all that is needed and seen in the Amish home. Since the styles and colors of the wearing apparel never change, a closet or dresser to preserve large varieties is not needed. The household goods can easily be secured at a sale or auction; style and age are of little consequence.

The greatest assets that the young people have are health and eagerness to work. Their aim is to save some money, so that eventually they may rent or buy a farm and move from a small unit to perhaps a quarter section of 160 acres, the ideal farm establishment in the area. Of work there is no end; the closely knit peasant society tolerates no wasting, and the parents will always be ready to help and advise so that the young people will come to success.

The first years of youthful exuberance may be exceedingly difficult. The man will probably not spare himself or his young mate, who besides her task of bearing and rearing children will often have to lend a hand in farm chores. The bloom of youth disappears quickly, and the woman will show the strain of her burdens more than will the man. However, married Amish couples often impress the modern city folk with an unusual peace and contentment which seem to be written into their faces and persons; one may well conclude that harmony of purpose rather than physical attraction gives their marriages solid foundation. A certain realism, quiet sobriety, a patient forbearance and stolidity in adversity and in the accidents of life soon engrave themselves into the Amish countenance.

The age at which the Amish marry seems to vary. In 1950 in Mifflin County, Pennsylvania, the mean age for Amish girls was 22.3 years, for boys 24.2 years. Dr. Maurice A. Mook discovered in Crawford County, Pennsylvania, that the mean age for Amish girls was 20.8 and for men 22.9 years.[6]

The announcement of intention to marry in the Sunday service terminates the secrecy so long affected and the whole district seems to rejoice and share in the anticipated event. It seems as if now "the game is up." All are happy, for so it is that independence has been won, a new family unit created, and the perpetuation of the community is assured.

Amish Wedding Days

Amish couples choose Tuesday or Thursday as their wedding day whether they live in Pennsylvania, Ohio, Indiana,

Iowa, or Florida. The pages of the Sugarcreek *Budget* amply confirm this statement. One Pennsylvania correspondent, in his own typical style, commented on the subject: "Rather unusual weather for the wedding season. Five were held on Tuesday. Many more on Thursday, some said ten, personally I doubt if there were that many. If there were that many it would be a record number for a single day."[7] The Amish wedding season lasts from early fall until late winter. For a wedding, the moon must not be on the wane. There are no weddings during leap year.

There are many reasons in an agricultural community for weddings to be held in fall and winter.[8] Even in European rural regions—for example, Bavaria and along the North Sea coast, as well as in the Scandinavian countries including Iceland—weddings are largely restricted to these seasons. Conditions favorable for the establishment of a new family unit are best estimated after the harvest. The productivity of the fields and farm and the available ready cash are then sufficiently known.[9] The young Amish couple may surmise future prospects from their newly joined efforts.

Such considerations are somewhat ephemeral and would base a marriage mainly on economic grounds. There are, obviously, more valid reasons for the fall weddings. After the summer's labors are completed, a time of rest and feasting presents itself. Diversion from farm chores is now appropriate and allowed in the strict sectarian community. While the Sunday district meeting does give some release to the Amish from the monotony and isolation of the daily routine, that observance alone is not enough. One might say that in fall three other diversions present themselves, to quote again a contributor to the *Budget:* "Farmers are butchering and attending sales and weddings." Another scribe wrote: "Quite a few are a-butchering this week. Hence not so many weddings a-going." This latter statement might lead one to believe that "a-butcherings" took precedence over weddings. Nevertheless, the close connection between the two is obvious, because the large number

of guests, usually between two and three hundred, will consume proportionate amounts of meat, as well as potatoes, bread, and cake.[10]

With the slackening of the work in barn and fields, the young married people find opportunity to become better acquainted. The young wife now has time to become the mistress of her household; at her own leisure she can learn to manage her kitchen and adapt herself to her husband's culinary tastes and domestic demands. Furthermore she is not yet embroiled in the ubiquitous sewing basket; nor need she spend her spare time mending and altering clothes. Time enough to visit the extensive circle of friends and relatives, upon whom it is obligatory to call, is also available. This is the Amish honeymoon. It is as important and perhaps more meaningful than the "Yankee" counterpart, because much advice and counseling passes on to young people who are receiving a kindly inspection and schooling tour. Aunts and uncles, who have grown strong in their Amish faith and are also successful farmers, have acquired much experience and wisdom worth sharing and passing on to new generations.[11] Then, with the coming of spring and the seasons of planting and growing, there is usually new life expected too; still, "in utero," the child has been present with all the work that is done on a non-machine operated farm; thus the child is a "born farmer."[12]

The Amish "wedding season" is, therefore, understandable and reasonable in its rural environment. In its rigidity and its failure to change, it is set apart from the American scene. Reasons for strict adherence to Tuesday and Thursday so far have defied all rational deciphering. The Amish pragmatic instinct crystallizes in the axiom: "Wenn man was unternimmt, muss man immer zuerst wissen, warum" ("if one undertakes something, one must always know first, why") does not seem to be applied when it comes to choosing only Tuesday or Thursday for weddings.[13]

The Amish do present acceptable arguments why a marriage cannot be on a Monday: The extensive preparations

185

for the district meeting, the housecleaning, cooking, and baking, the arranging of tables for the many guests cannot be done on Sunday, the Lord's day and a literal day of rest. A wedding held on Tuesday has at least one day's advantage, and the bride and her parents have a chance to prepare a satisfactory, generous feast. The wedding in both religious service and secular aspects must run smoothly. The opposite would only be to the discredit of the bride according to the Amish estimate: "A sloppy wedding makes a sloppy bride."[14] No young Amish woman would want to have this said of her. If this is so, then one would guess that Wednesday and Friday were days more advantageous. Strange to say, however, neither day does come into consideration. Only Thursday is still available. It is easy to see that Thursday is to be preferred to Tuesday when it comes to the labor involved for preparation. The exclusion of Saturday one may justify from the Amish point of view, because this day is generally one of preparation for the Sunday with its religious meeting. A wedding held on Saturday might leave the house untidy for Sunday, a condition, as noted before, simply not tolerated.

In the firm adherence to Tuesday and Thursday, Amish reasoning itself is strained beyond the breaking point and is at war with itself. But these folk have never questioned the validity of the custom. In this tradition the Amish have preserved an ancient culture pattern of which they are aware without knowing its age or significance.

(It is important to observe here, too, that the Amish move to a new farmstead, rented or bought, only on Thursday. Some of their own members are baffled as to the reason moving takes place only on Thursday. Nevertheless, moving day is Thursday.)

The Amish have here preserved for modern society the clear traces of ancient pagan cults which pre-date the Christian era, cults based upon the worship of the pre-Christian Germanic gods, Ziu and Donar. In this, more than in any other phase of their distinctive life, the Amish form a cultural enclave, stronger and more cohesive than any other one known within modern America.

The search for an explanation of the two-day limitation on weddings so far has proved fruitless among the Amish themselves. The most honest answer one may obtain from them only admits that "Amish traditions are deep rooted. Some are based upon some (right or otherwise) interpretation of scripture. Some is plain folk custom. Some border hard on superstition."[15] The latter statement is a concession rarely forthcoming from an Amishman. An Amish informant of wide travel and experience hinted at a possible clue when he ventured a guess saying he believed it was on those days that in olden times "they did not hang people." This surmise came closer than he knew, while at the same time he intimated a deep historical significance.

For the proper understanding of the Tuesday-Thursday wedding tradition, it is necessary to recall that the supreme gods of the Germanic peoples, Ziu or Tiu and Donar or Thor, are still perpetuated in our present English and German day names, *Tuesday* and *Thursday*. The Amish of course use a derivative German in their daily discourse, and the English *Tuesday-Thursday* are the German *Dienstag-Donnerstag*. Tuesday is named for Ziu or Tiu, the highest god of the Germanic peoples, the god of heaven and war. His equivalent in Greece was Zeus and in Rome, Jupiter.[16] On the other hand, Thursday, Donnerstag, is named for Donar or Thor, who was not only the god of power and might, as witnessed in his manifestations of thunder and lightning, but also the god of the earth and the weather, the protector and source of strong family pedigrees, the guardian of the home; along with Ziu, moreover, Donar was the maintainer of right and justice and the vindicator of injustice.[17] Court was held and contracts were made under the aegis of these two gods, and the favorite terms for all contractual agreements were the days dedicated to them. In the Nordic lands the *thing*, the people's assembly, was

187

held on Thursday, and in Switzerland until comparatively recent times court convened on this day.[18]

The gods Ziu and Donar had in their custody the home and every newly founded family, and they were particularly the deities of matrimony. Once upon a time Tuesday was the favorite wedding day, as Tuesday, god Ziu's day, had always been regarded a lucky day.[19] Many superstitions and practices are still associated with this day, although the reason for such behavior is now generally forgotten. Enterprises begun on this day, especially when related to the home and farm, were assured of success. In ancient times marriages held on Tuesday were protected against all evil influences, especially against witchcraft, because they stood under the tutelage of the noblest and highest god, Ziu.[20]

Thursday is the preferred day for weddings in certain rural sections of Germany, in the Alpine regions, in Friesland, Dithmarsum, Pomerania, and in Holland. In rural South Germany one can still hear it said today: "Donnerstagsheirat—Glücksheirat" ("Thursday's wedding—lucky wedding"). Here the god, Donar, was the pre-eminently revered god of marriage, and of course it must be added that he is the god of agriculture, of the livestock, and of fertile growth. Practically all farm life and increase was his special domain.[21]

It is important to know that the Church, in order to undo the worship and cults of the pagan gods upon the Christianization of the Germanic peoples from about the sixth century on, fought some of its most valiant battles. Prohibitions and injunctions alone could not bring acquiescence. Thus, some of the highest feasts of the Church were laid upon pagan holy days. The most noted example of course is Christmas, in which the birth of the Saviour was laid into the Germanic holy season of the winter solstice. To transform the cult of Donar, the Church placed some of its most solemn and memorable events upon Thursday, as, for instance, the Last Supper, Ascension, and above all Corpus Christi, Europe's highly ostentatious religious festival, resplendent with all the possible pomp a city or community can muster, coming at a time when nature has attained its fullest beauty. What could not be eradicated was thus given a Christian interpretation.[22] Yet deep in the heart of the people remained some of its most cherished and ingrained practices, the most significant of which is marriage, as the German word *Hochzeit* (high [time] tide) itself so adequately implies. The reverence shown by simple, earth-bound people like the Amish to Tuesday and Thursday is an ineradicable and unmistakable remnant of former worship cults of the ancient gods which neither the medieval Church nor the modern age have been able to undo.[23]

Ancient and medieval Christian arguments militating against the use of the other days of the week as wedding days may also be of interest. The name *Monday* implies that the day is named after the moon, the emblem and embodiment of inconstancy and fickleness. Besides its variableness, the moon is also an element of the night, of darkness, of furtiveness of things and actions that fear the light of day, scrutiny, and truthfulness. Anything of a lasting nature was not begun on Monday. German folk wisdom expresses this conviction in such common sayings as (translated): "Monday grows not a week old," or "Monday's beginning lasts not long," and "Rough Monday, smooth week."[24] Perhaps more valuable and consequential among religious folk than these facts is the implication derived from the work of creation, as recorded in the Book of Genesis. The Lord did not say at the end of the first day: "And it was good." Transferred into everyday life this meant that activities begun on this day of the week had no particular sanction. A wedding of course is not to be held on Monday. Moreover the common belief brands "Monday's children are unlucky children."[25]

In the name *Wednesday*, English preserves the name of the Germanic god Wodan. His was a holy day in ancient times. The Christian church, in order to undo the memory

189

of Wodan, stamped Wednesday-Wodansday as a day of misfortune, for was it not on this day that the greatest misfortune befell Christianity, the betrayal by Judas? Wednesday, in the conflict between paganism and Christianity, became the Devil's day, and Christianity won the battle. No one, thereafter, would have dared to put the most important even in the life of two young people on this day; their future would be foreordained to unhappiness. The young bride was sure to return to her parents or the couple would never be able to finish their chores if they should be married on this day.[26]

Friday likewise overflows with evil omens and taboos. The death and misfortune of Christ on the cross was too sad a memory for the beginning of any serious enterprise. The adage "Was Freitags wird begonnen, hat nie ein gut' End genommen" ("Whatever is begun on Friday has never taken a good end") sums up in concrete formula the character, temperament, feelings, customs, and actions of the countryfolk concerning this day. Even in modern society, Friday still holds a certain sway over the minds of men. It is reported of Napoleon that he would not commence a battle or draw up a contract on this day. Similar allegations are also made of Bismarck.[27] In a few rural sections of Germany, Friday was, however, a favorite wedding day, equal to Tuesday and Thursday because this day, as the very name implies, was dedicated to the goddess Freya, the Germanic Venus. In most sections it is avoided as an unlucky day; in certain Alpine regions even courting and visiting are avoided on this day.[28]

The Christian church apparently had nothing evil to say about either Tuesday or Thursday. Nothing objectionable in the story of man's salvation as recorded in the New Testament could be assigned to these two days. While Sunday was advanced by the Church as a preferred day,[29] nevertheless one possible wedding day was not sufficient for a people so closely bound to nature and to an anthropomorphic interpretation of its setting within this nature. The Amish themselves seem to have permitted only one Sunday wedding, and the circumstances under which it occurred were singular and forced upon them by modern economic life. The one Sunday wedding, which occurred in Ohio during World War II, was necessitated by the groom's employment in an industrial concern in the city. It seems he could not take a day off from his work.

The Amish have preserved for us cult practices of ancient, pre-Christian times and, in continuation, will remain a link with the past, so easily lost by modern Americans.

MARRIAGE

The most joyous social event in the lives of the Old Order Amish is the marriage festival. In its woof and weave the Amish wedding is such a noble, solemn, and complex arrangement that it stands unique in the cultural pattern of America. It signifies the culmination and also the cessation of parental influences, the declaration of growth and independence, and a renewal of life cycles. There is woven into this feast a strange mingling of Christian and pre-Christian elements, of religion and superstition, of folk wisdom and demoniac fears, so that one stands awed by this observance within modern time.

The custom of sending the favored preacher of the young couple to the girl's parents to inquire whether the groom is suitable and acceptable to them has lost its significance today. The parents are well aware of the associations and intentions of their daughter, and, in addition, it would be too late to object. Some elders bemoan the disappearance of this item of Amish life, and its former importance seems unquestioned. The Old Testament story of the wooing of Abraham stands precedent for it. The Pennsylvania word *Schteckleimann* for *solicitor*, the word for Abraham's servant, is hardly known here in Ohio. Some Amish seem to recall the word but not the meaning and connection. In former times, the "Schteckleimann" also carried the young man's proposal to the girl and subsequently invited the guests to the feast; these missions are no longer customary. The bride invites the guests by mail.

The size of the girl's home and, more often, the number of her relatives determines the number of invited guests. If the house is too small, a neighbor's or even the boy's home may be used for the festivities; the girl's parents, however, are still responsible for food and its preparation. All the bride's relations are invited, from married brothers and sisters and their families to grandparents, aunts, uncles, and first cousins. Neighboring farmers, Amish and non-Amish, and perhaps the employers for whom the girl may have worked in the city are also invited. The groom's guests are often confined to the members of his immediate family. Weddings have an added social significance, because they reunite relatives from remote parts of the country. Young people from distant states may come and look for mates; but in some respects wedding feasts become legitimate excuses for the Amish love of travel. There is a record of a busload of thirty-one guests coming to an Ohio wedding from a neighboring state. It is understandable that hats, hoods, shawls, and boots are easily interchanged; one sympathizes with the pointed advertisements in the Sugarcreek *Budget* for a good hood which had been substituted for a shabby one and for an all wool bonnet which had been exchanged for an old one after a wedding.

The choice of guests may make or break a friendship of long standing. Permanent likes and dislikes take their origin from such deliberations. The reputation of the girl's parents remains at stake, and it is most important that they know who is invited. Much consideration is therefore given to the list of guests. It is not unusual to find between sixty and seventy families or between two- and three-hundred people at a wedding celebration. That this is really a great holiday within the Amish community can also be surmised from one particular instance: when the daughter of a well-to-do Amish man was married, the nearby Amish parochial school was more than half empty.

The elaborate preparations for the feast demand the help of many hands. Not only does the bride's family often paint the outside of the house and barns but the inside of the home, from bedrooms to the basement larder, is sometimes refurbished. Everything is scrubbed, washed, polished. Days and weeks go into the preparation. The groom moves into the house several days before the appointed date. His two "mates" or "witnesses," either brothers, cousins, or best friends, usually selected in this order, arrive the day before the wedding. They give as much time as possible to helping prepare the tables. The two bridesmaids are also present; they may be sisters, cousins, or friends. They, too, help with food preparation and kitchen chores, and these helpers stay to help restore the home after the celebration.

On the wedding day, three young men, the "hostlers," are responsible for seeing that the bridal party reaches the meeting place where the ceremony is to be performed. The hostlers drive the party of three couples in three buggies, which are polished and painted for the occasion. The horses and buggies of the guests are also in the care of the hostlers. Their last official function is to pass a jug around when dinner and supper are underway, and their success in their tasks is judged by the amount of noise and the change they may extract from the guests. This collection is distributed among the cooks and waitresses who are usually cousins of the bride.

The propitious American warning to the bride, "something old and something new," is unknown in the Amish country. The apparel of both bride and groom however often is new for the day, the groom wearing a homemade blue serge suit, with either blue or white collar-less broadcloth shirt underneath. The bride wears a freshly ironed, light blue, cotton dress with high neckline and full skirt, with a white net organdy kerchief and apron reaching from the neck to the full length of the skirt; on her head for the last time is the black prayer cap. She wears a dress similar to her daily costume in color, material, cut; she has no veil, no flowers or prayer book. The attendants, moreover, look exactly like the bride and groom. The bridal couple is recognized only by their position between the attendants. The two male attendants keep the groom in their midst, as do the two maids the bride. Should they walk about or be driven to and from the meeting place, the bridal couple is preceded by one of the attending couples and followed by the other. By outer appearance bride and groom cannot be distinguished from their respective attendants. This manner of keeping bride and groom unrecognizable and carefully guarded seems an unconscious Amish concession to primitive fears of hostile, predatory influences. The Amish call the two male and female attendants "witnesses" in English. Their dialect names them *nevvehocker*; in High German, *Nebenhocker*; or, in English translation, "Those who squat beside."

The marriage ceremony is always held in a separate home from that in which the guests are entertained at dinner. The religious service compares in outer form with a regular Amish district meeting. The guests arrive between nine and ten o'clock in the morning. Together they sing appropriate hymns and selected stanzas from the *Ausbund*. The quality of the music does not differ from other Amish singing. While the congregation is thus occupied in the lower part of the house, the bride and groom in an upstairs room receive final instructions in the ideals and duties of husband and wife toward each other in Amish married life. This meeting with the church officials is called *Vermahnung* ("exhortation"). The attendants await the bridal couple at the stairway. Later they conduct the pair to the center of the meeting, where they sit opposite each other and near the officiating church leaders.

Two sermons are preached, as upon regular meeting days. The theme of the sermons is matrimony, and the two

194

preachers, chosen by the bride and groom from among their favorite preachers in the region, will extol most of the married people found in the Scriptures. The first preacher usually dwells on those from Adam and Eve to Ruth or the Flood; his successor will continue to the story of Tobias, consuming all of two hours. Some regard is paid to the time, so that the service does not go much beyond one o'clock, and the cooks at home usually plan on that hour. It is assumed the wedding will last all day, and no one seems in a hurry to go anywhere else.

The marriage rite itself is remarkably brief. It consists, in part, of promises which young people generally make to each other in the presence of preachers, witnesses, and the whole community. It also employs the only such rite found in the Scriptures. In putting the hands of the spouses together and pronouncing his blessing over them, the bishop uses verbatim Verse 15 from the seventh chapter of the apocryphal Old Testament book, Tobias. The marriage becomes a Christian rite only by the addition of the words: "And all this through Jesus Christ. Amen."

The ceremony proper follows the second sermon, the preacher having finished the story of Tobias. Now the bishop of the district invites the bride and groom to stand before him. He directs these few questions to them in German (here translated by the author from a text supplied by an Amish bishop):

"Do you also recognize it as a Christian Order that there should be one man and one woman, and can you hope too that you have started this union according to the Christian Order?"

"Yes."

"Can you too hope, brother, that the Lord might have ordained this our sister as a married wife?"

"Yes."

"Can you too hope, sister, that the Lord might have ordained this our brother as a married husband?"

"Yes."

195

"Do you promise to your married wife, that if she should come into bodily weakness, sickness or any kind of condition that you will care for her as is becoming a Christian married man?"

"Yes."

"Do you promise to your married husband, that if he should come into bodily weakness, sickness or any kind of condition that you will care for him as is becoming a Christian married woman?"

"Yes."

"Do you both also promise to the Lord and to the community that you will bear with each other love, life [Leib] and patience and not separate from one another until the dear Lord will part you through death?"

"Yes."

Thereupon the bishop takes the right hand of the woman and puts it into the right hand of the man, praying and saying:

"So we see that Raguel took the hand of the daughter and put it into the hand of Tobias and said: The God of Abraham, the God of Jakob, the God of Isaac be with you and help you together and give you his blessing richly over you, and all this through Jesus Christ. Amen."

Now the newly married persons resume their former places opposite each other and between their witnesses.

Joining of the hands by the highest authority in the community, the bishop, is the official marriage act, and his prayer and blessing mark the culmination of the marriage ceremony. There are, of course, no altars, lighted candles, no incense, no holy water, no flowers, no white carpets, nor pillows to kneel upon, as there are no ring, no veil, no kiss, no gloves, no crown, no bouquet, no public demonstration of affection to mar or interrupt the holy rite. The married couple does not rush out of the meeting place. Instead all those present join in the Lord's Prayer. As is also customary in the fortnightly meeting, the male guests may hold forth in the form of testimonials concerning the married state or biblical precedents. Symbolic of Amish life and the position they assume in it, the women do not speak up. Similarly the bride allows the groom to answer first the questions addressed to both by the bishop.

The Old Order Amish church, as such, does not issue certificates and keeps no records. Until recently members of the sect did not even record their marriage in the county courthouse. The laws of the State of Ohio did not require civil registration if a marriage had been duly announced and published in the Sunday service. In the middle nineteen-fifties civil and hygienic registration became compulsory in Ohio. The Amish, without exception, seem to comply with the new ordinances.

Strangely enough, the parents of the bride do not attend the marriage service of their daughter. They remain at home supervising the arrangements of the dinner so that guests will find ample pleasure and refreshment.

The wedding dinner initiates the secular festivities of the day. The spread of food upon the long tables is a gastronomical treat, superabundant and fulsome. Tradition and precedent have cast their mark upon the variety of food presented. One wedding dinner is reported in which a bride of twenty-seven years of age had all the dishes in varieties of sevens, to encourage good luck. Otherwise custom has it well established that the three best dishes are included in the noon dinner: a meat dish, usually chicken, but sometimes the proverbial fatted calf, veal, plus mashed potatoes and a "stuffing" of some sort. A warm sausage dish may be added to this. Then there are cold cuts, cheese, celery stalks, cole slaw, bread, butter and apple butter, pickles, and canned fruits and cookies. Angel food cake for dinner and loaf butter cake for supper are served as desserts. For supper there are only two hot dishes, meat loaf and noodles, or ham and noodles, besides the other cold dishes of the noon meal. There are endless amounts of food and service, and no limits to time. The dinner lasts until late in the afternoon, unless there are two or even three shifts to be

served. The food is never taken off the table, but any empty platters are refilled from the kitchen larder. Anyone may eat as much and as long as he desires. Cold dishes stay on the table for the evening meal. From this a midnight snack is available for those who are still about. Wine may be served by the groom only to his immediate party of the *nevvehocker*, according to biblical precedent.

The bridal party is separated from the other guests in this way: the wedding party sits in the extreme corner of the room with the bride occupying the right side of the corner, the groom the left, so that they half face each other. Next to the bride sits her best girl friend, and the groom has his best friend beside him. The other attendants sit on the outside. Initialed and decorated cookies usually serve as place cards. A punch bowl in the nature of a cornucopia, or "horn of plenty," filled by the bride with a selection of sixes —six apples, six oranges, six bananas, six bunches of grapes, six candy bars, six chocolate bars, six packages of chewing gum—decorates the dinner table. The bride will distribute this treat to each of her immediate wedding party and her new husband on the day after the celebration. This bowl is quite modern and forbidden in some districts. Each couple also has in front of it a large bowl of fruit and jello. The bridal party may be favored by a special meat dish, perhaps a roast chicken, and usually a double or triple decker fancy cake.

The bride's father has one special prerogative commensurate with his acknowledged authority: he shows the guests to their places, although the dinner may not be at his own home. Her mother supervises the affairs of the kitchen. The guests sit by age groups, the younger ones nearer the bridal party. The older people are also segregated by sexes. The married men and girls sit at the large living room table. The married women eat in the kitchen; the young boys eat wherever there is room. One special table, often in a different room, is set for the preachers, bishops, and singers.

The meal is begun with silent prayer, but it ends with singing. When there is a lull in the eating, each dinner guest brings forth his book of century-old songs. Only the bride and the groom do not sing, so as not to weep tomorrow. The Amish monotone singing seems to have a sobering rather than an exhilarating effect. It is now that the guests may leave the banquet hall and move about to inspect the farm. The older people often remain in the house to talk farm and community problems, the unmarried and younger married may go to the barn where the upper floor has been cleaned to provide space for genuine barn or square dancing. Now the groom may go about to greet the guests and to offer cigars or candy bars. He may even receive a money gift in return for this favor.

Presentation of the wedding gifts to the bride and groom is made after the evening supper. Each guest appears, as a rule, opposite the newlyweds, and with appropriate words he tries to justify and make merry about the practical gift he has selected. This probably makes for the greatest merriment of a rather realistic nature, because each guest now has a chance to say what he has long prepared to say to the new couple. For example, one groom reveived a "big steel wheelbarrow with the purpose of cleaning out his cow stable in case the farm he gets has no litter carrier in." If the guest is a relative of the groom, he has probably selected something useful for him in the barn or farm, like pitchfork, spade, carpenter tools, hammer and nails, broom, axes and saws, or milking buckets. Since most of the guests are relatives of the bride, she naturally receives the largest number of presents, all welcome and necessary in home and kitchen. Because of the German proverb: "Einem geschenkten Gaul sieht man nicht ins Maul" ("one does not criticize a present"), the bride does not object to items which the strict Amish code does not favor, as for instance glassware with painted flowers, dishes with designs, linen with embroidery. While she admires the gift and the giver, her emotions are often mixed when gifts are destined to be put into a corner cupboard rather than to be put to work. Sometimes the guests even try to embarrass newlyweds by giving gifts for a baby; the Amish community, like any other, is not free from gossipy tongues who wait to decipher whether the marriage was an emergency or a genuinely free choice.

With lighthearted merrymaking the evening wears on. The older folks gradually remove to their own homes, the younger set stays to frolic in the barn. Toward midnight this rollicking begins to quiet down. After most of the guests have departed, the bridal couple retires to its own seclusion in the house. The "witnesses" also stay overnight.

A honeymoon in the accepted American sense is unknown in Amishland. It is not unusual, however, that the newlyweds, shortly after the wedding day go a-visiting and make the rounds of their many relatives, spending a day or two with each. An interesting account of the day after the celebration appeared in the Sugarcreek *Budget:*

> Along with hunting, November is also the open season for weddings among the Amish. . . . The ceremony took place at the home of the bride's uncle, where the happy couple spent their wedding night. As is custom among the Amish, so they tell us, the newlyweds were required to do the family washing the next day, and complications usually arise as friends remove parts of the washer or loosen the washline, hide the clothes pins and wash props, or anything that will make their first attempt a tough one.

> "Well, the couple started out bravely enough the next morning, and after a real struggle the line was soon sagging under plenty of clothing until ——— happened along. . . . loosened the line and the whole shebang hit the ground. ——— managed to elude detection for a time by hiding in the ——— home, but when he attempted to escape he was captured by a

number of the men and forced to climb the pole to replace the line.

While he was still up the pole, struggling with the balky line, his shoes were removed and filled with good, soft, cozy mud from the barnyard, and his face neatly painted with rich, black shoe polish. And ——— still looked like a coal miner on a holiday later when he attended another wedding in the same section.

When all is over the parents will find that the wedding day's entertainment was a costly one in effort and money; the latter is estimated to be between five and six hundred dollars. Most families keep a detailed record of expenses and quantities of food consumed; this is done more carefully when there are other daughters to follow. If there is more than one daughter, the father also does well to buy the lumber and build the dining tables to fit into the downstairs of his house, and then store them away until the next event. The simple wooden benches owned by the district and used in its regular meeting also serve here. However, the family's reputation has not suffered a setback, for "a full stomach is also a contented stomach," and the new couple with the approval of satisfied relatives, members of the community, and the leaders of the districts involved has been started off in the right manner. How could it be otherwise?

The Amish marriage rite is still a family and communal affair, as characteristic of peasant society as it was of medieval Germany in the days of *Meier Helmbrecht* in the thirteenth century. Here the mores connected with marriage seem untouched and altogether forgotten by the progress of the ages; indeed it seems as if Western civilization had made a circuitous march around them. To describe them is like unveiling a bygone scene or like undigging an archeological past. One can find no basis for comparison between the modern American marriage, extravagant and showy, with emphasis on clothes, flowers, church appointments, with the simple if lengthy Amish observance; the latter remains almost entirely a religious and folk rite, its participants unworldly and unsophisticated. The only thing one can say is that both take place in the mid-twentieth century, separated in space only by a few short miles.

CONCLUSION

The author is often asked the question: Are the Old Order Amish in Ohio increasing or decreasing? Paradoxically, one must answer both yes and no. From small beginnings one-hundred and fifty years ago, the Amish have come to occupy a large part of the rural area of Wayne and Holmes counties. The number of Old Order members, however, has not increased as much over the years as one might expect from the reported size of Amish families. For the years, 1958–59, the latest available figures, the Old Order group in east-central Ohio did not record any growth in its membership.

While modernized methods of transportation and farming have indeed won noticeable defections in the struggle between tradition and progress, Amish growth and virility nevertheless remain vigorous. The local Ohio group is simply unable to absorb its own increased population. According to recent news accounts, Wayne County Amish have explored the possibility of settling in Alaska and some have already located in the middle and western provinces of Canada. A few Amish farmers have sold their Ohio land to relatives and moved east to certain mountain valleys of Pennsylvania, there to be less exposed to the influences of the "world." Some of these venturers have returned, finding the religious climate in the Keystone state incompatible with the mode of life they had known in Ohio.

The Amish are able to absorb some of their increasing numbers by dividing their farms. This enables them to preserve their manner, if not necessarily their standard, of living. In this process, the soil becomes insufficient to support the growing family, and agriculture comes to offer only part-time occupation, leaving many working hours to be filled by other pursuits. The problem of the scarcity of land contains grave threats to the Amish way of life. Several methods of meeting the disparity between increase in numbers and the scarcity of farm land have been mentioned. In addition, some younger families have begun to restrict the number of their offspring.

But the most portentous of the threats to the Amish way of life lies in the trend toward part-time employment in the cities which the insufficiency of their farms makes necessary. This cityward tendency foreshadows the possible abandonment, by the men and families involved, of the rural life. The danger is manifest in the inconsistencies so noticeable in Amish behavior. Worldly means of making a living are accepted for economic reasons, while they are rejected in the Amish community itself. An Amish carpenter, for instance, on a city job, employs electric power saw and drill. After curfew, however, within his own rural environment the possession of these tools is forbidden. A father who travels by rented car or in a car pool to the city may be led finally to surrender to the desire of sons who recognize both auto and city as means to a superior way of living and earning.

The Wooster city telephone directory bears witness that some Old Order Amish have abandoned the rural life and its accompanying restrictive faith. Only three of the forty-three Amish family names listed by Deacon Ervin Miller (chap. ii) are not listed in Wooster. These three names—Bontrager, Helmuth, and Nisley—are also rare in the Amish community. On the other hand, three most common Amish names—Miller, Yoder, and Troyer—overrun the Wooster directory, with Miller by far the most frequent name in the county seat. A few of these city families belong to the local Mennonite church or Mennonite churches in the county. The majority, however, are members of liberal Protestant denominations. Some of the city dwellers with typical Amish names may not be of Mennonite descent, of course.

Sporadically metropolitan newspapers print accounts of Amish families on the move with horses, wagons, and all tangible possessions. The reasons are purported to be the stringent Ohio school law which compels boys and girls to attend school until the age of sixteen and social security regulations, which now embrace all agricultural workers. The second most frequent question then is this: Are the Amish leaving Ohio because of these laws? The author finds that the implication of this question—that all Amish may be leaving Ohio—is simply not true. While these reasons may apply in given instances, neither school laws nor the extension of social security has produced any large-scale shifts in Ohio Amish population. There have been only isolated, sensational cases which the press has accentuated. It should be stressed again that during the whole history of the Amish in Ohio relocations and migrations have been perpetual features of their existence. To reiterate: The most compelling motive for migration, in the past as in the present, is the availability of cheaper and more abundant tillable land elsewhere.

The Old Order Amish have always found ways of adapting themselves to the cultural climates around them. Yet it is likely that the economic and social forces engulfing them in twentieth-century America are stronger than anything Old Order Amish conservatism has had to contend with in the past. The Amish boy or young man who has once worked in a city factory or on a modern, motorized farm will hardly be convinced later that salvation results from milking a cow by hand, not waking the laying hen by electric light, or from fattening a steer by muscular rather than mechanical devices. When he becomes harness maker for his neighbors in the faith, he will accommodate his knowledge and his faith by installing four or five small gasoline engines to work his various machines, electrical motors being taboo; as cobbler for his group some similar motor will move his cutting and polishing machinery.

The Old Order Amish community in America may become the last refuge of German peasantry. In Germany the accentuated rate of modernization, communication, and transportation is causing the rapid disappearance of the "Bauer." The so called "*Wirtschaftswunder*," the miracle of economic revival on the Continent, is pervading even the most remote rural areas. The German "Bauer," who a scant twenty years ago believed that his horse or ox and his fractional parcels of land were his eternal, foreordained inheritance is of a different mind now. The changes and mechanization all about him are strong propagandists, and rural and city inhabitants will not for long show sharp cultural and social differences.

When the author, upon the invitation of the United States government, lectured to German audiences about the German contributions to America, they were astonished to know that in America a German-type "Bauer" had developed who in language, appearance, bearing, thinking, and behaving was preserving the traditions of the Old World with utmost tenacity. From another point of view, the Old Order Amish are a revelation to Europeans because they have succeeded in maintaining a distinct "group" character in an America renowned for modernity and progress and an apparent homogeneity and conformity in manners and customs. Europeans ordinarily do not suspect that a group like the Amish, free in its hilly surroundings to preserve an age long gone, can exist in America. The Amish must then become increasingly attractive to the student of Old World folkways: what escapes the researcher abroad may be alive in America, not as a festival-day exhibition but as the very core of Amish being.

This, in part, answers the third most frequently heard question: What will become of the Old Order Amish in Ohio? Without assuming the role of either seer or prophet, the answer is simple. There will always be Old Order Amish, barring international catastrophe. This claim needs no complicated justification. The people of the hilly backroads of east-central Ohio live relatively sheltered and unmolested. Furthermore, as Anabaptists and Mennonites, they have a long history of survival behind them. As the "first sect of Protestantism" with origins in Reformation times, the doctrines of these religious agriculturists have developed deep, tough roots. The large number of Mennonites in modern America attests to their vigor and vitality. The followers of Menno Simons and Jakob Ammann were among the earliest settlers of German stock after 1683 in Germantown, Pennsylvania. In Ohio the Old Order Amish have had an unhindered existence until comparatively recently. From pioneer ventures in 1807 they have increased, in spite of defections by individuals and by groups, to some forty districts in this region. Their negative attitude toward many American opportunities acts as a brake on their growth but will not destroy them.

The Old Order Amish and their tenets require no defense in an America jealous of its own liberty, dedicated to preserving individualism, and zealous in rigorous separation of church and state. Every shade of Christian interpretation and exploration augments the religious health of this nation and adds weight to the purposes of the founding fathers. The Old Order Amish, and all the other groups which have sprung from them, have contributed permanently to the national religious kaleidoscope.

As this investigation of the Amish in Ohio began with an observation made at the beginning of the nineteenth century by the poet, Schiller, in his *William Tell*, so the eulogist of Swiss life may supply the close for this study. In Act II, scene 1, of *William Tell*, a young man, Rudolf, attracted by the gay world of the imperial court, debates with his uncle, Attinghausen, lord of the manor and one-time leader of his peasant warriors. The conflict which Schiller ascribes to the thirteenth century is the conflict today in Ohio. Rudolf asks:

> Think you. . . . That I should loiter,
> Here on the heritage my fathers left,
> And in the dull routine of vulgar toil? . . .

Attinghausen replies:

> The world asks virtues of far other stamp
> Than thou hast learned within these simple vales . . .
> Cling to the land, the dear land of thy sires,
> Grapple to that with thy whole heart and soul.
> Thy power is rooted deep and strongly here. . . .
> This foreign witchery, sweeping o'er our hills,
> Tears with its potent spell our youth away! . . .
> O luckless hour! When men and manners strange
> Into these calm and happy valleys came,
> To warp our primitive and guileless ways.
> The new is pressing on with might. The old,
> The good, the simple, fleeteth fast away.
> New times come on. A race is springing up,
> That think not as their fathers thought before!

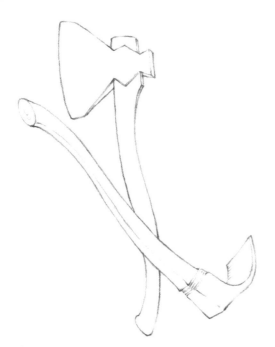

NOTES

CHAPTER 1

1. Article VI of the Ordinance of 1787, quoted in Ben Douglass, *History of Wayne County* (Indianapolis, Ind., 1878), p. 23.
2. Caleb Atwater, *A History of the State of Ohio, Natural and Civil* (Cincinnati, Ohio, 1838), p. 352.
3. Douglass, *op. cit.*, pp. 183, 185.
4. *Ibid.*, p. 654.
5. Atwater, *op. cit.*
6. Henry Howe, *Historical Collections of Ohio* (Cincinnati, 1848), p. 237.
7. *Ibid.*, p. 427.
8. Douglass, *op. cit.*, p. 849.
9. *Ibid.*
10. B. F. Brown, *A History of Wayne County, Ohio* (2 vols.; Indianapolis, Ind., 1910).
11. *Ibid.*, I, 375.
12. In 1959.
13. J. C. Wenger, *The Doctrines of the Mennonites* (Scottdale, Pa., 1950), Appendix I, p. 71.
14. *Ibid.*, Appendix III, p. 87.
15. David A. Treyer, *Hinterlassene Schriften* (2d ed.; Arthur, Ill.; 1925), p. 69.
16. J. S. Umble, *Ohio Mennonite Sunday Schools* (Goshen, Ind., 1941), pp. 94–95.
17. Joseph W. Yoder, *Amish Traditions* (Huntington, Pa., 1950), p. 56.
18. Treyer, *op. cit.*, pp. 156 ff.
19. *Ibid.*, p. 56.

CHAPTER 2

1. Benjamin Rush, *An Account of the Manners of the German Inhabitants*, as quoted in C. J. Bachmann, *The Old Order Amish of Lancaster County* (Norristown, Pa., 1942), p. 239.

2. Ralph Ely, "A History of the Amish People of East Union Township, Wayne County, Ohio" (Master's thesis, Ohio State University, 1942), chap. iv, pp. 1 ff.

3. Karl Weinhold, *Die Deutschen Frauen in dem Mittelalters* (Wien, 1882), II, 297.

4. Ervin Gingerich, *Ohio Amish Directory* (Millersburg, Ohio, 1959), Vol. I.

5. E. W. Burgess and H. J. Locke, *The Family* (New York, 1945), p. 69.

6. This expression is used by C. G. Bachmann in his *The Old Order Amish of Lancaster County* (Norristown, Pa., 1942), p. 90.

7. Cf. Mary Jane Hershey, "A Study of the Dress of the (Old) Mennonites of the Franconia Conference, 1700–1953"(Master's thesis; reprinted in *Pennsylvania Folklife*, Summer, 1958).

8. Joseph Yoder, *Amish Traditions* (Huntington, Pa., 1950), p. 129.

9. H. Howe, *Historical Collections of Ohio* (Cincinnati, 1848), p. 257.

10. Don Yoder, "Plain Dutch and Gay Dutch," *The Pennsylvania Dutchman*, Summer, 1956, p. 40. Cf. Don Yoder, "The Costumes of the 'Plain People,'" *The Pennsylvania Dutchman*, March, 1953.

11. *Op. cit.*, p. 40.

12. *Ibid.*, pp. 25 ff.

13. *Ibid.*, p. 29.

14. Bachmann, *op. cit.*, p. 88.

CHAPTER 3

1. John Umble, "The Old Order Amish, Their Hymns and Hymn Tunes," *American Folklore*, III (January–March, 1939), 82.

2. *Ibid.*

3. *Ibid.*, p. 92.

4. *Meier Helmbrecht* ll. 186–90, as quoted in Johann Schwendimann, *Der Bauernstand im Wandel der Jahrtausende* (Köln, 1945), p. 234.

CHAPTER 5

1. L. A. Miller, *Handbuch für Prediger* (Scottdale, Pa., 1950), pp. 7 ff.

2. *Ibid.*, pp. 18–25.

3. *Ibid.*, pp. 19, 22.

4. *Ibid.*, pp. 21, 24.

5. *Handbuch*, p. 39.

6. Cf. H. S. Bender, "The First Edition of the Ausbund," *Mennonite Quarterly Review*, III (April, 1929), 147–50.

7. The Amish churches of Lancaster County, Pa., own the plates of this edition of 3,000 copies. The 14th edition of 4,000 copies came off the press late in 1958. This probably means that there will be no revisions in the text for some time to come.

8. This type of singing by the "Vorsänger" carries over into modern songs as well. Amish children in the parochial school use it, for instance, in singing "Silent Night," which a boy or girl will lead in every verse:

> *Sti*lli Nawcht, heili Nawcht.
> *Alles* schlawft, einsam wawcht,
> *Nur* das trauti, heili Pawr
> *Das* da in dem Stalli wawr.
> *Schlawf* in himmlichi Ruh,
> *Schlawf* in himmlichi Ruh.

9. Joseph K. Yoder, *Amische Lieder* (Huntingdon, Pa., 1942).
10. George P. Jackson, "The Strange Music of the Old Order Amish," *The Musical Quarterly*, XXXI (July, 1945), 284–85.
11. William I. Schreiber, "The Hymns of the Amish Ausbund in Philological and Literary Perspective," *Mennonite Quarterly Review*, XXXVI (January, 1962), 36–60.

CHAPTER 6

1. The *Budget* of the calendar year 1949 provided the basis for the present analysis. Names of individuals, apart from first names, are omitted. Otherwise, items are given as in the original.
2. "Cooperation Builds a Barn in a Day," *American-German Review*, XVI (August, 1950), 18–19. This event took place August 4, 1949, at Ben Weaver's place near Mt. Hope, Wayne County, Ohio.

CHAPTER 7

1. H. Brockmann-Jarosch, *Kiltgang im Emmental* (Basel, 1931), II, 83.
2. H. R. Stiles, *Bundling* (Harrisburg, Pa., 1928), pp. 30 ff.
3. Trans. and ed. by H. S. Bender, as "An Amish Bishop's Conference Epistle of 1865," *Mennonite Quarterly Review*, XX, No. 3, pp. 227, 228.
4. David A. Treyer, *Hinterlassene Schriften* (2d ed.; Arthur, Ill.), pp. 64–65.
5. *Op. cit.*, p. 67.

6. John A. Hostetler, "Recent Textual Treatment of the Amish," *Mennonite Quarterly Review*, XXV, No. 2, 1951, p. 136.
7. William I. Schreiber, "The Amish Sugarcreek *Budget*," in *The Morning Call* (Allentown, Pa.), January 5 and 12, 1957. All references to the *Budget* are from this article, an analysis of Amish life as revealed in the weekly newspaper during the calendar year 1949.
8. Cf. Karl Weinhold, *Die Deutschen Frauen in dem Mittelalter* (Wien, 1882), II, 363.
9. Cf. Otilie Doll, *Mir Dean Heirat'n: Eine Untersuchung über die Bäuerliche Gattenwahl in Bayern Südlich der Donau und Nebst Anschliessenden Randgebieten* (München, 1940), pp. 44 ff.
10. The Amish affirm P. Sartori's treatment of the wedding "als Gemeindeangelegenheit" in "Hochzeit," in *Sachwörterbuch der Deutschkunde*, ed. Walther Hofstaetter and Ulrich Peters (Berlin, 1930), I, 546 ff.
11. Similar customs are cited by Hanns Bächtold, *Die Gerbräuche Bei Verlobung und Hochzeit mit Besonderer Berüchsichtigung der Schweiz* (Basel, 1914), I, 14.
12. Cf. Doll, p. 48.
13. Cf. K. F. W. Wander, *Deutsches Sprichwörterbuch* (Berlin, 1876), IV, 1480: "Wer unternimmt, was er nicht versteht, kommt mit Schaden davon."
14. This proverb was supplied by a Wayne County, Ohio, informant who wants to remain anonymous.

15. This quotation is from a letter to the author of August 15, 1956, by an Amishman who prefers not to be named. However, his remarks closely approximate those of R. Beitl in his *Deutsche Volkskunde* (Berlin, 1933), p. 164: "Die Hochzeit ist in ihrem inneren und äusseren Verlauf ein so vielgestaltiges und edles Gebilde volkstümlicher Lebenskunst, dass wir es uns nicht versagen können, an Hand von einigen kundigen und treuen Berichten zu betrachten, wie sich diese höchste Lebensfeier in ihrer seltenen Mischung von Glauben und Aberglauben, Weisheit und Dämonenfurcht, urvolklich-heidnischen und christlichen Vorstellungen—wie sich eine rechte Hochzeit im engeren Zusammenhang einer einzelnen Landschaft, eines besonderen Volksstammes vollzieht."

16. Cf. Karl Simrock, *Handbuch der Deutschen Mythologie* (Bonn, 1855), Par. 87, pp. 315 ff.; and Friedrich von der Leyen, *Deutches Sagenbuch*, Vol. I: *Die Götter und Göttersagen der Germanen* (München, 1909), p. 96.

17. Cf. Simrock, *op. cit.*, Par. 78, pp. 277 ff.; von der Leyen, *op. cit.*, pp. 158 ff.; and Weinhold, *op. cit.*, I, 375.

18. See Jungbauer, in Hoffmann-Krayer's *Handwörterbuch des Deutschen Aberglaubens* (Berlin, 1929–42), s.v. "Dienstag," II, 249 ff., and s.v. "Donnerstag," in II, 331 ff.

19. Kurt Heckscher, *Die Volkskunde des Germanischen Kulturkreises*, Part II: *Volksglauben* (Hamburg, 1925), Par. 155, pp. 254.

20. Cf. Weinhold, *op. cit.*, I, 364, with literature for diverse parts of Germany.

21. Cf. G. Buschan, *Das Deutsche Volk in Sitte und Brauch* (Stuttgart, 1922), p. 152; Jungbauer, *Handwörterbuch*, II, 339. Donar is designated by Weinhold, *op. cit.*, I, 375, as "Ehegott"; by Simrock, *op. cit.*, p. 281, as "Gott der Ehe"; and by von der Leyen, *op. cit.*, p. 96, as "Gott der Bauern."

22. See Jungbauer, *Handwörterbuch*, s.v. "Donnerstag," II, 333; Kummer, *Handwörterbuch*, s.v. "Hochzeit," IV, 171–73; Sartori, *Handwörterbuch*, s.v. "Fronleichnam," III, 120 ff.

23. Cf. H. Barthel, *Der Emmenthaler Bauer Bei Jeremias Gotthelf Ein Beitrag Zur Bäuerlichen Ethik* (Münster in Westfalen, 1931), p. 31, where he treats marriage as "Abschluss und Höhepunkt der Jugend." See also Buschan, *op. cit.*, 154.

24. These three proverbs are also found in Wander, *op. cit.*, III, 218–19.

25. Cf. Weinhold, *op. cit.*, I, 360; Jungbauer, *Handwörterbuch*, s.v. "Montag," VI, 554; Otto Laufer, *Niederdeutsche Volkskunde* (Leipzig, 1923), p. 88.

26. See Jungbauer, *Handwörterbuch*, s.v. "Mittwoch," VI, 433 ff.; Wein-

hold, *op. cit.*, 336: "Mittwoch ist überhaupt ein Unheiltag oder wenigstens kein Ehrentag."

27. See Jungbauer, *Handwörterbuch*, s.v. "Freitag," III, 52.

28. Cf. Jungbauer, *Handwörterbuch*, III, 56; Weinhold, *op. cit.*, I, 367;

Heckscher, *op. cit.*, Par. 155, p. 354.

29. Cf. Jungbauer, *Handwörterbuch*, s.v. "Sonntag," VII, 88 ff. For the church's attitude toward Sunday weddings, see also Weinhold, *op. cit.*, I, 365.

SELECTED BIBLIOGRAPHY

ALLGÄUER, E. "Vom Liebesleben unseres Landvolkes," in *Heimat: Volkstümliche Beiträge zur Kultur und Naturkunde Voralbergs.* Innsbruck, 1922.

Amish Sectarian Education in Ohio. (Research Report No. 44.) Columbus, Ohio: Ohio Legislative Service Commission, 1960.

APEL, WILLI. *Harvard Dictionary of Music.* Cambridge, Mass., 1945.

ATWATER, CALEB. *A History of the State of Ohio, Natural and Civil.* Cincinnati, 1838.

Ausbund das ist Etliche schöne Christliche Lieder. 13th ed. Lancaster County, Pa., 1955.

BACHMANN, C. J. *The Old Order Amish of Lancaster County.* Norristown, Pa., 1942.

BÄCHTOLD, HANNS. *Die Gebräuche bei Verlobung und Hochzeit mit besonderer Berücksichtigung der Schweiz: Eine vergleichend volkskundliche Studie.* Vol. I. Basel, 1914.

BARTELS, ADOLF. *Der Bauer in der deutschen Vergangenheit.* Leipzig, 1900.

BARTHEL, HELENE. *Der emmenthaler Bauer bei Jeremias Gotthelf.* Münster, 1931.

BAUER, THERESE. *Das oldinger Jahr: Brauch und Sitte im Bauernstand.* Erfurt, 1944.

BECKER, ALBERT. "Kirche und Volkstum: Zur kirchlichen Volkskunde der Pfalz," in REIHE, *Beiträge zur Heimatkunde der Pfalz.* Zweibrücken, 1933.

BEITL, R. *Deutsche Volkskunde.* Berlin, 1933.

BENDER, H. S. "An Amish Bishop's Conference Epistle of 1865," *Mennonite Quarterly Review,* XX (July, 1946), 222–29.

BENDER, H. S. "The Anabaptist Vision," *Church History*, XIII (March, 1944), 3–24.

———. "The First Edition of the Ausbund," *Mennonite Quarterly Review*, III (April, 1929), 147–50.

———. "Literature and Hymnology of the Mennonites of Lancaster County, Pennsylvania," *Mennonite Quarterly Review*, VI (July, 1932), 157–68.

———. *Mennonite Origins in Europe*. Akron, Pa., 1945.

BERGMANN, KARL. *Die Ehe in der Auffassung der Deutschen mit besonderer Berücksichtigung des Sprichwortes*. Darmstadt, 1940.

BLOHM, GEORG. *Bäuerliche Lebensordnung*. Posen, 1944.

BOWEN, B. F. *History of Wayne County, Ohio*. 2 vols. Indianapolis, Ind., 1910.

BRACHT, THIELEMAN, J. VAN. *Martyrs' Mirror*. Scottdale, Pa., 1938.

BROCKMANN-JEROSCH, H. "Kiltgang im Emmenthal," *Schweitzer Volksleben*. Basel, 1931.

BRUNIER, I. W. *Das deutsche Volkslied*. Leipzig, 1908.

BURGESS, E. W., and LOCKE, H. J. *The Family*. New York, 1945.

BUSCHAN, G. *Das deutsche Volk in Sitte und Brauch*. Stuttgart, 1922.

COFFMAN, S. F. (ed.). *Mennonite Confession of Faith*. Scottdale, Pa., 1957.

CORRELL, ERNST H. "The Sociological and Economic Significance of the Mennonites as a Culture Group in History," *Mennonite Quarterly Review*, XVI (July, 1942), 161–66.

———. "The Value of Hymns for Mennonite History," *Mennonite Quarterly Review*, IV (July, 1930), 215–19.

DÖRRER, ANTON. "Das 'Gasslgehn' ging im 'Fensterln' auf," *Ammann Festgabe II, Innsbrucker Beiträge zur Kulturwissenschaft*. Vol. II. Innsbruck, 1954.

DOLL, OTTILIE. *Mir Dean Heirat'n: Eine Untersuchung über die bäuerliche Gattenwahl in Bayern südlich der Donau und nebst anschliessenden Randgebieten*. Munich, 1940.

DOUGLASS, BEN. *History of Wayne County, Ohio*. Indianapolis, Ind., 1878.

DÜRINGFELD, IDA VON. *Hochzeitsbuch: Brauch und Glaube der Hochzeit bei den christlichen Völkern Europas*. Leipzig, 1871.

ECKENS, HEINKE. *Die Lage der Bauern nach Ihrer Befreiung in Deutschland*. Graz, 1959.

ELY, RALPH. "A History of the Amish People of East Union Township, Wayne County, Ohio." Unpublished Master's thesis, Ohio State University, Columbus, Ohio, 1942.

ERK, LUDWIG C., and BÖHME, FRANZ M. *Deutscher Liederhort*. 3 vols. Leipzig, 1883–94.

FEHRLE, EUGEN. *Deutsche Hochzeitsbräuche*. Jena, 1937.

FISCHER, J. G. *Schiller's Works*. 4 vols. Philadelphia, 1883.

FREY, J. WILLIAM. "Amish Triple Talk," *American Speech*, XX (April, 1945), 85–98.

FRIEDMANN, ROBERT. *Mennonite Piety through the Centuries: Its*

Genius and Its Literature. Scottdale, Pa., 1949.

FUNK, J. F. *Confession of Faith and Minister's Manual.* 9th ed. Scottdale, Pa., 1942.

GASCHO, MILTON. "The Amish Division of 1693–1697 in Switzerland," *Mennonite Quarterly Review,* XI (July, 1937), 235–66.

GINGERICH, ERVIN. *Ohio Amish Directory.* 1959, 1960.

GLICK, NETTIE. *Historical Sketch of the Walnut Creek, Ohio, Amish Mennonite Church.* Scottdale, Pa., 1933.

GOEDEKE, KARL, and TITMANN, JULIUS. *Deutsche Dichter des 16. Jahrhunderts.* 3 vols. Leipzig, 1867.

GOLDMANN, EMIL. *Hochzeitsgebräuche und Seelenreise.* Vienna, 1956.

GRABERT, HERBERT. *Der Glaube des deutschen Bauerntums: Eine weltanschauungskundliche und glaubensgeschichtliche Untersuchung,* Vol. I, *Bauerntum und Christentum.* Stuttgart, 1939.

GRATZ, DELBERT. *Bernese Anabaptists and Their American Descendants.* Scottdale, Pa., 1953.

GUENTHER, FRANZ. *Kleine Geschichte des deutschen Bauerntum.* Oldenburg, 1958.

GÜNTHER, HANS F. K. *Das Bauerntum als Lebens und Gemeinschaftsform.* Leipzig, 1939.

HABERLANDT, ARTHUR. *Die deutsche Volkskunde: Eine Grundlegung nach Geschichte und Methode im Rahmen der Geisteswissenschaften.* Halle, 1935.

Handbuch für Prediger. Scottdale, Pa., 1950.

HANSEN, WILHELM. *Das deutsche Bauerntum. Seine Geschichte und Kultur.* Vols. I and II. Berlin-Schöneberg, 1938.

HECKSCHER, KURT. *Die Volkskunde des germanischen Kulturkreises.* 2 vols. Hamburg, 1925.

HELM, RUDOLF. *Die bäuerlichen Männertrachten im Germanischen Museum zu Nürnberg.* Heidelberg, 1932.

HERSHEY, MARY JAMES. "A Study of the Dress of (Old) Mennonites of the Franconia Conference, 1700–1953." Master's thesis, Drexel Institute of Philadelphia, 1957. Reprinted in *Pennsylvania Folklife,* Summer, 1958, pp. 24–47.

HILDENBRANDT, BRIGITTE. *Nachtigallen zu Hausvögel machen.* Hamburg, 1958.

HOFFMANN-KRAYER, E. *Handwörterbuch es deutschen Aberglaubens.* Vols. I–X. Berlin, 1927–42.

HORSCH, JOHN. *The Hutterian Brethren: A Story of Martyrdom and Loyalty, 1528–1931.* Scottdale, Pa., 1931.

———. *Mennonites in Europe.* Scottdale, Pa., 1942.

HOSTETLER, JOHN A. "Amish Costume: Its European Origins," *American-German Review,* XXII (August, 1956), 11–15.

———. "Recent Textual Treatment of the Amish," *Mennonite Quarterly Review,* XXV (April, 1951), 133–36.

———. *The Sociology of Mennonite Evangelism.* Scottdale, Pa., 1954.

Houet, A. l'. *Psychologie des Bauerntums.* Tübingen, 1935.

Howe, Henry. *Historical Collections of Ohio.* Cincinnati, 1848.

Jackson, George Pullen. "The Strange Music of the Old Order Amish," *The Musical Quarterly,* XXXI (July, 1945), 275–88.

Jobst, Albrecht. *Evangelische Kirche und Volkstum: Ein Beitrag zur Geschichte der Volkskunde.* Stuttgart, 1938.

Keller, Ludwig. *Geschichte der Wiedertäufer.* Münster, 1880.

Koch, Georg. *Die bäuerliche Seele.* Berlin, 1935.

Koch, Hermann. *Ich Bauer bin das Volk.* Berlin, 1940.

Kohl, F. F. "Die tiroler Bauernhochzeit," *Quellen und Forschungen zur deutschen Volkskunde,* Vol. III. Vienna, 1908.

Kolesch, Hermann. *Deutsches Bauerntum im Elsass.* Tübingen, 1941.

Kollmorgen, Walter M. *Culture of a Contemporary Rural Community: The Old Order Amish of Lancaster County, Pennsylvania* ("Rural Life Studies, No. 4.") Washington, D.C.: U.S. Department of Agriculture, 1942.

Laedrach, Walter. *Das emmenthaler Bauernhaus.* Bern, 1941.

Laemmle, August. *Brauch und Sitte im Bauerntum.* Berlin, 1935.

Laireiter, Mathias. *Die Grundlagen der bäuerlichen Existenz.* Salzburg, 1959.

Langel, A. *Trachten und Sitten im Elsass.* Strassburg, 1902.

Lauffer, Otto. *Niederdeutsche Volkskunde.* Leipzig, 1923.

Leers, Johann. *Odal: Das Lebensgesetz eines ewigen Deutschland.* Goslar, 1936.

Leyen, Friedrich von der. *Deutsches Sagenbuch,* Vol. I, *Die Götter und Göttersagen der Germanen.* Munich, 1909——.

Littell, Franklin H. *The Anabaptist View of the Church.* New York, 1952.

Mast, John B. *Eine Erklärung über Bann und Meidung.* 1949.

Mennonite Encyclopedia. 4 vols. Scottdale, Pa., 1955–59.

Mennonite Historical Bulletin. Scottdale, Pa., 1940——.

Mennonite Life. North Newton, Kansas, 1945——.

Mennonite Quarterly Review. Goshen, Ind., 1924——.

Mennonite Yearbook and Directory. Scottdale, Pa., 1905——.

Mielke, Robert. *Der deutsche Bauer und sein Dorf.* Weimar, 1942.

Miller, Emanuel J. *Jeremiah Miller Family History.* Wilmot, Ohio, 1943.

——. *Joni Miller Family History.* Wilmot, Ohio, 1942.

Miller, Jakob. *Deutsche Bauerngeschichte.* Stuttgart, 1941.

Miller, L. A. *Eine Begebenheit die Sich in der Mennoniten-Gemeinde in Deutschland und in der Schweiz von 1693 bis 1700 zugetragen hat.* Arthur, Ill., 1936.

Mook, Maurice A. "Extinct Amish Mennonite Communities in Pennsylvania," *Mennonite Quarterly Review,* XXX (October, 1956), 267–76.

Neckel, Gustav. *Liebe und Ehe*

bei den vorchristlichen Germanen. Leipzig, 1932.

PEACHEY, PAUL. *Die sociale Herkunft der Schweizer Täufer in der Reformationszeit.* Karlsruhe, 1954.

PETER, ILKA. *Gasslbrauch und Gasslspruch in Österreich.* Salzburg, 1953.

PFEFFER, K. H. *Der Bauer: Bücher zur deutschen Volkskunde.* Leipzig, 1939.

RABER, J. A. *Artikel und Ordnungen der christlichen Gemeinde in Christo Jesu.* Baltic, Ohio, 1954.

———. *Der neue amerikanische Calender.* Baltic, Ohio, 1929———.

RADBRUCH, RENATE MARIA. *Der deutsche Bauernstand zwischen Mittelalter und Neuzeit.* Munich, 1941.

RAMAKER, A. J. "Hymns and Hymn Writers among the Anabaptists of the Sixteenth Century," *Mennonite Quarterly Review,* III (April, 1929), 93–131.

RECHENBACH, HORST. *Bauernschicksal ist Volkesschicksal.* Berlin, 1935.

RETZLAFF, HANS. *Bauernhochzeit im Elsass.* Berlin, 1937.

———. *Deutsche Bauerntrachten.* Berlin, 1934.

RIEHL, WILHELM HEINRICH. *Die Naturgeschichte des deutschen Volkes,* ed. GUNTHER IPSEN. Stuttgart, 1939.

RUMPF, MAX. *Das gemeine volk: Ein soziologisches und volkskundliches Lebens—und Kulturgemälde in drei Bänden,* Vol. II, *Religiöse Volkskunde.* Stuttgart, 1933.

RUNGE, F. W. *Das Buch des deutschen Bauern.* Berlin, 1935.

SAHR, J. *Das deutsche Volkslied.* Leipzig, 1908.

SARTORI, PAUL. *Sitte und Brauch.* 3 vols. Leipzig, 1910–14.

SCHEDA, KARL. *Deutsches Bauerntum: Sein Werden, Niedergang und Aufstieg.* Reutlingen, 1934.

SCHEIDLE, JOSEF. *Bauernbüchlein.* Innsbruck, 1936.

SCHELLINGER, A. *Das bäuerliche Jahr.* Karlsruhe, 1939.

SCHOLZ, HUGO. *Welt des Bauern.* Breslau, 1936.

SCHREIBER, GEORG. *Deutsche Bauernfrömmigkeit in volkskundlicher Sicht.* Düsseldorf, 1937.

———. *Die Wochentage im Erlebnis der Ostkirche und des Christlichen Abendlandes.* Cologne, 1959.

SCHREIBER, WILLIAM I. *The Fate of the Prussian Mennonites.* Göttingen, 1955.

SCHULTZ, B. K. *Bäuerliche Lebensgemeinschaft.* Leipzig, 1940.

SCHWENDIMANN, JOHANN. *Der Bauernstand im Wandel der Jahrtausende.* Cologne, 1945.

SIMROCK, KARL. *Handbuch der deutschen Mythologie.* Bonn, 1855.

SMITH, C. HENRY. *The Education of a Mennonite Country Boy.* Bluffton, Ohio, 1943.

———. *The Mennonite Immigration to Pennsylvania in the Eighteenth Century.* Bluffton, Ohio, 1929.

———. *The Mennonites: A Brief History of Their Origin and Later Development in Both Europe and America.* Berne, Ind., 1920.

———. *The Story of the Mennonites.* Berne, Ind., 1941.

SMITH, E. L. *The Amish People: Seventeenth-Century Tradition in*

Modern America. New York, 1958.

SMITHSON, R. J. *The Anabaptists: Their Contribution to Our Protestant Heritage.* London, 1935.

SMUCKER, DONOVAN E. "Anabaptist Historiography in the Scholarship of Today," *Mennonite Quarterly Review,* XXII (April, 1948), 116–27.

SPIESS, KARL. *Deutsche Volkskunde als Erschliessung deutscher Kultur.* Berlin, 1934.

SPRINGENSCHMID, KARL. *Die Bauernwelt: Grundlagen bäuerlichen Wesens.* Worms, 1958.

STAUFFER, ETHELBERT. "The Anabaptist Theology of Martyrdom," *Mennonite Quarterly Review,* XIX (July, 1945), 178–214.

STILES, H. R. *Bundling.* Harrisburg, Pa., 1928.

STOLTZFUS, GRANT M. "Cooperation Builds a Barn in a Day," *American-German Review,* XVI (August, 1950), 18–19.

STROBEL, HANS. *Bauernbrauch im Jahreslauf.* 2d ed. Leipzig, 1937.

STUCKEY, HARLEY J. "The Agricultural Revolution of Our Day," *Mennonite Life,* XIV (July, 1959), 117–21.

TREYER, DAVID A. *Hinterlassene Schriften. Unter welchen sind auch mehrere erbauliche und geistreiche Gedichte zum Druck übergeben von seinen Kindeskindern.* Arthur, Ill., 1925.

TROELTSCH, ERNST. *Die Soziallehren der christlichen Kirchen und Gruppen.* Tübingen, 1912.

UHLAND, LUDWIG. *Alte Hoch- und Niederdeutsche Volkslieder.* 2 vols. Stuttgart, 1866–81.

UMBLE, JOHN. *Ohio Mennonite Sunday Schools.* Goshen, Ind., 1941.

———. "The Old Order Amish: Their Hymns and Hymn Tunes," *Journal of American Folklore,* LII (January, 1939), 82–95.

———. "Recent Research in Amish Hymn Tunes," *Mennonite Quarterly Review,* XXIV (January, 1950), 91–93.

WACH, JOACHIM. *Sociology of Religion.* Chicago, Ill., 1946.

WACKERNAGEL, PHILIPP. *Das deutsche Kirchenlied.* 5 vols. Leipzig, 1864–77.

WANDER, K. F. W. *Deutsches Sprichwörterbuch.* 5 vols. Berlin, 1867–80.

WEBER, HARRY F. *Centennial History of the Mennonites of Illinois, 1829–1929.* Goshen, Ind., 1931.

WEIGERT, JOSEPH. *Religiöse Volkskunde, ein Versuch.* 3d ed. Freiburg, 1925.

WEINHOLD, KARL. *Die deutschen Frauen in dem Mittelalter.* 2 vols. 2d ed. Vienna, 1882.

WENGER, JOHN C. *The Doctrines of the Mennonites.* Scottdale, Pa., 1950.

———. *Glimpses of Mennonite History and Doctrine.* 2d ed. Scottdale, Pa., 1947.

———. (ed.). *Menno Simons: Complete Writings.* Translated from the Dutch by LEONARD VERDUIN. Scottdale, Pa., 1956.

WIKMAN, K. ROB. V. *Die Einleitung der Ehe. Eine vergleichend eth-*

nosoziologische Untersuchung über die Vorstufe der Ehe in den Sitten des schwedischen Volkstums. Abo, 1937.

WOLKAN, R. Die Lieder der Wiedertäufer. Berlin, 1903.

WOOD, RALPH. The Pennsylvania Germans. Princeton, 1942.

YODER, JOSEPH W. Amische Lieder. Huntingdon, Pa., 1942.

———. Amish Traditions. Huntingdon, Pa., 1950.

———. The Prayer Veil Analyzed. Huntingdon, Pa., 1954.

———. Rosanna of the Amish. Huntingdon, Pa., 1944.

———. Rosanna's Boys. Huntingdon, Pa., 1948.

YODER, SANFORD C. For Conscience Sake: A Study of Mennonite Migrations Resulting from the World War. Scottdale, Pa., 1940.

ZALLINGER, OTTO. Die Ringgaben bei der Heirat und das Zusammengeben im mittelalterlich-deutschen Recht. Vienna, 1931.

ZIEGLSCHMID, A. J. F. Die älteste Chronik der hutterischen Brüder. Philadelphia, Pa., 1943.

INDEX

225

Meyer, Jacob C., 29
Middle District Conference, 26
Military service, 33, 57, 80–81
Miller, Eli J., 79–86, 117
Miller, Isaac I., 97, 102, 103, 104
Miller, Jacob (Jockle), 17
Miller, John C., 145
Millersburg (Ohio), 65, 66
Mills, Edwin, 114
Missions, foreign, 34–35; see also Charities
"Mite"; see "Meidung"
Mores; see Adaptation; Customs
Mougey, Walter J., 103, 109–11, 112
Music, 121, 174; see also Hymns

Names, 37, 56 f., 147
Neue Amerikanische Calender, Der, 130
Neuenschwander, Michael, 18–19
Newkirk, John and Reuben, 15
New Amish, 26
Nisley, John J., 97, 102, 103, 104, 107, 108, 109, 113–14, 117

Oak Grove Mennonites, 26–28, 29
Oath taking, 33
Ohio Amish Directory, 37
Old age, 39; see also Grandparents
Old Mennonites, 26
Old Order Mennonites, 25, 30
Old Order Wisler Mennonites, 26
Ordinance of 1787, 10, 11
Ordination of leaders; see Leaders
"Ordnung" and "Gebrauch"; see Customs
Orphans, 39, 129

Patriarch, father as, 57–58
Peasant: mentality, 39; traditions, 61, 87–92; see also "Bauer"
"Pennsylvania German" dialect, 3

"Plain people," 60
Plenary district meeting, 124
Preaching, 3, 4, 35, 40, 122–23, 124–25, 131, 164, 194–95
Pride, 83–84, 92, 179

Quakers, 65

Raber, J. A., 130
Read, Robert, 113
Recreation, 33, 168, 173–74
Reformed Mennonites, 26
Regulations; see Law; State and federal regulations
Remarriage, 156
Ritual; see Marriage; Weddings; Sunday service
Rural environment, 22, 29, 39, 75, 123, 149, 150
Rush, Benjamin, 52–53

Sabbath, 119–20
St. Clair, Arthur, 12
Salvation, 40, 58, 131, 135
Schiller, Friedrich, 9, 208
Schisms, 19–20, 22, 27, 28, 57
Schleitheim Confession of Faith, 31, 75, 124, 130–31
School bus, 55; see also Lentus Bus Line
Schools, 38–39, 54–55
Schraag (Schrock), Benedict, 18
Schwarzendruber, Jacob, 179
Swartzentruber district, 26, 39
Scriptural basis of Amish faith, 76, 79–86, 122, 130
Separation, 31–33, 34–37, 39, 40–41, 54, 81–83, 123; of church and state, 4–5
Sermons; see Preaching
Settlement, 17, 18, 24, 38, 43–44, 47, 164–65